Multicultural Marketing Is Your Story

Multicultural Marketing Is Your Story

Eliane Karsaklian

BUSINESS EXPERT PRESS
Leader in applied, concise business books

Multicultural Marketing Is Your Story

Copyright © Business Expert Press, LLC, 2023.

Cover design by Charlene Kronstedt

Interior design by Exeter Premedia Services Private Ltd., Chennai, India

First published in 2023 by
Business Expert Press, LLC
222 East 46th Street, New York, NY 10017
www.businessexpertpress.com

ISBN-13: 978-1-63742-469-8 (paperback)
ISBN-13: 978-1-63742-470-4 (e-book)

Business Expert Press Marketing Collection

First edition: 2023

10 9 8 7 6 5 4 3 2 1

Description

Ever since *Homo sapiens* populated our world, our lives have been stories we tell to all those we are surrounded by every day as well as to unknown people through social media when we post the pictures of our vacations, pets, children, and graduation or changes in our jobs. We buy brands that have a story we admire or those that are recommended by influencers because we are fascinated by their stories.

This book is about you. It is the story of your past, your present, and your future as you live in multicultural communities. Page after page, you see the story of humankind and of multiculturalism unfold and be explained through the lenses of science and storytelling.

Multicultural Marketing Is Your Story is thoroughly illustrated with real-life examples. The ideas, theories, and statements presented in this book will perhaps challenge some of your deepest beliefs or they might as well comfort you in your own opinions. Ultimately, this book is an invitation to reflection, to critical thinking, to objectivity, and to the liberty of accepting what is different.

Keywords

multiculturalism; multinational; storytelling; social media; tribes; science; culture

Contents

Acknowledgment

I would like to address my recognition to Dr. Naresh Malhotra for his guidance and precious recommendations when reviewing my manuscript.

Introduction

What's the Story?

This book tells the story of the influence of culture on consumers ever since *Homo sapiens* populated our world. Everything that is told in the following pages is based on scientific research and on the author's first-hand multicultural experience. Because we are storytellers and story consumers, this book explores multicultural marketing from the stories consumers tell and are told about products and brands.

Indeed, our lives are stories we tell to all those we are surrounded by every day. We tell stories about our lives to unknown people too through social media when we post the pictures of our vacations and when we share about our graduation or changes in our jobs. We add videos of our pets, of our wedding dance, and of our newborn and their first steps. We don't even wonder if someone else is interested in our lives; we just want to be on the spotlight (for free). And we can immediately know if our story was well accepted, shared, or rejected, thanks to the number of views, likes, comments, and shares.

We like the stories Netflix and their competitors tell us. We go to the theater to hear the stories the actors perform. We read (audio) books to ourselves and to others. We watch the news to see and hear the stories told by journalists, we listen to music to hear the stories told by the composers, and we visit museums to enjoy the stories told by artists in their paintings and sculptures.

We are storytelling consumers. We buy brands that have a story we admire and we willingly buy the brands recommended by influencers because we are fascinated by their stories. We are storytellers and story consumers. And this talent started centuries ago when people would gather around the fire to tell stories. Stories are the oldest way of communication and persuasion. In marketing, advertising, brands, and logos tell stories to consumers (Karsaklian 2012). And it is because we can relate to their stories that we buy those brands.

Ultimately, storytelling is the use of words that can make an impact on listeners and in all cultures, people tell stories, although each culture has their own stories rooted in their past. In fact, culture itself is a story. Think of culture as a sequence of events within a structure just like a movie. Sometimes you get in without knowing the characters; sometimes it starts in the present time and takes you back to the past to explain where the present situation is coming from and you see the actors evolving and adapting their behavior to specific situations as the story unfolds. It is the authors' job to depict the underlying reasons leading the characters to behave the way they do.

This is also the way you start interacting with people from other cultures without having studied their culture beforehand. We ask ourselves questions but the answers are often delayed or hard to find. Sometimes, our questions remain unanswered. And we wonder what is going to happen next. It is intriguing, disruptive, and sometimes threatening. Actions drive stories, which are the roots of any culture (history), roots in which cultural values are grounded. Actions are in the heart of interactions, and interactions are what disclose cultural differences, help create memories, and forge connections.

More than being storytellers, we have always been multicultural storytellers. Because we have always lived in a multicultural world, each tribe around the world would have their own stories to tell. Later, we started sharing them through writings and arts—followed the humans' direct interactions with other tribes thanks to migration movements, colonization, and globalization.

Any Cause Can Look Plausible When the Story Is Well Told and Addresses Emotions

No story is credible without a context. No story makes sense without a context, a structure. There are places, characters, and scenes in all stories. And stories differ because of the context—and this context is often culture. Thus, when we listen, understand, and adopt some of the stories from other cultures, we become multicultural.

We understand multiculturalism when we understand context and relativism. Everything in nature is relative. And everything has a context in which it is generated and grown. What makes you who you are is not the color of your skin or your country of birth. Your race is biological and your country of birth might not be the country you were raised in. What shapes your mind, your values, your beliefs, and your behavior is where you were socialized and by whom you were raised.

As we grow up, we are taught the language, behavioral patterns, religious beliefs, and all the dos and don'ts to live in that specific society. This is how we become who we are. And when we move to another country, we need to learn about their specific patterns in order to be part of their society because all societies are different. In other words, culture is contextual.

Everything in the world is contextual. Only the understanding of context can enable sense-making. Context makes everything relative and relativism creates different perspectives to the same thing. When events of any kind are taken out of context, they become absolute rather than relative and are narrowed down to only one possible interpretation of them. This can cause despair in a multicultural world. Our perceptions and thus our interpretations of the same event are different because of our cultural differences.

Centuries ago, Newton stated that the notion of time and space was absolute but to Einstein it was relative. This can be explained by the fact that determinism takes events out of context while relativism puts them into context, that is, it gives perspective to them. Because Newton was a classical physicist, his theories followed determinism. But Einstein was a quantum physicist and his theories were based on relativism, his most famous one being the theory of relativity. Likewise, Maxwell stated that electricity and magnetism were different things and that light was static. Einstein proved that an electromagnetic field exists and that it is dynamic. Just like cultures, the study of natural phenomena is subjected to contextual interpretation and evolves with time.

Einstein's theories sounded absurd at the beginning but ended up being adopted by all physicists. Likewise, whenever you state something that looks counterintuitive or different (opposed) to the main beliefs, you are considered a liar or an ignorant. But if people checked the facts that you are demonstrating, they would see that you were right and that they should have fact-checked before. Rather, they believe in any plausible story and spread it out as if it were the absolute truth.

The Waves of 0.4/0.7 Micron Are Visible to the Eyes While the Infrared and Ultraviolet Are Invisible. Yet, They Exist

People tend to believe only in what they see but what they see might not be real. And what they can't see can hit them very hard. We see scenes in movies but they are not real. Yet, they are able to trigger emotions. But if you ask people whether rainbows are real they will say that they are not because we can't touch them yet they can see and admire them. Whether tangible or intangible, visible or invisible, there are several factors that shape our behavior and culture is one of those invisible things that shape our existence.

Although rainbows are a natural and universal phenomenon, their interpretation varies according to the culture. In Roman mythology, they were thought as the path taken by a messenger between earth and heaven. To the Irish, they are a sign of good luck and have a pot of gold guarded by Leprechauns at the end of the arc. And in Peru, they are associated with malign spirits, so people traditionally avoid them to be safe of illness dissemination.

Nothing is definitive and scientific understanding of natural phenomena evolves every day. Such evolution is meant to enlighten our brains and help us live in a better world by reducing ignorance. Perceptions are subjective and interpretations are personal. That is why knowing and understanding are fundamental. Science teaches us to never take anything for granted.

For example, when we have a great time playing with snow, building snowmen, and getting involved in snowball fights, we don't realize that snow is protons spinning in the earth's magnetic field. We cannot know it without measuring it. It is when we measure with extreme accuracy that we make great discoveries. Culture is not different. The deeper your understanding of a culture, the more accurate will your interpretation of it be.

The lack of measure leads to assumptions and companies often fail internationally because they assume rather than measure. What is called "details" and are frequently neglected because of a "lack of time" can hide or explain a whole lot of phenomena. When we study cultures, we know that both the invisible and the salient have the same relevance. Multiculturalism helps to understand the world by first understanding human behavior. Culture only discloses its properties to the ones who understand it. You need to be culturally curious (Karsaklian 2017) if you want to understand multiculturalism.

Multiculturalism rests on cultural curiosity, on openness to cultural diversity, and on the willingness to know about one's and others' cultures. Multiculturalism is the opposite of blind following; it is the understanding that cultural differences exist, that they are enriching and go far beyond biological traits. Multiculturalism is an invitation to get out of one's own cultural group to explore others' cultures.

The more we understand a culture, the more intriguing and fascinating it turns out to be. There is no amazement without analysis and understanding. You can't feel excited when you don't know what you are doing. How to be passionate if what you think and do doesn't come from you? Each discovery is a window toward something new and different. It is progress. We all have access to the same information. Some just take it as is, but some others go beyond it. What we do with that information is what makes all the difference. The ones who do things differently are often criticized, rejected, and set apart. But when they succeed in their endeavors, they are admired and followed.

People Like Stories That Balance Adventure and Stability

There is nothing easier than following and being part of the same mob. Anyone can do the obvious, repeat mechanically what is said by others, behave like others, and live through others. It is much easier than facing their own reality every day. It is easier than making the effort of standing out (the obvious doesn't stand out) and taking the risk of defending their own ideas and ideals which might differ from the mainstream ideas. It is both comfortable and frustrating—comfortable, because there is no need to worry about adaptation, criticisms, and rejection when we are part of a mob, but frustrating because deep down we know that we are not contributing to the evolution of cultural knowledge including our own. We also know that we are not contributing to our personal evolution as human beings.

It is hard to be on one's own, look in the mirror, and see that we are alone. We were not set up to live alone and our culture is what brings us together. So many contacts in the virtual life for so much loneliness in the real life. It is terrifying because identifying and accepting the flaws of our culture and the admiration of other cultures means breaking the very structure of our reality before rebuilding it in a new and improved form. It's painful and highly disturbing. Thus, following the mob and refraining from giving a different opinion keeps people safe: safe from cancellation. They are frustrated but at least they are not canceled. Even when they are unsure about the pertinence of the cause they are defending and the authenticity of the story they have been told, they will join the mob, to avoid the embarrassment of explaining themselves to others.

Yet, frustration comes when we realize that the cause was not legitimate—so much effort, time, and money for something that was not, in reality, what we were told. We are upset because we fell for that story. This is when we feel silly and regret having not analyzed the situation before hand. Beliefs are not facts. Likewise, in the Middle Age, it was believed that light came from objects or from our eyes. It took centuries before we understood that these are just the reflections of real sources of light such as the sun. We then realized that there were other valid hypotheses than the one that became prevalent at that time.

Further studies and experiments demonstrated that light moves faster in the air because there is less resistance than in denser environments such as water and some other materials; density creates resistance. Just like light, ideas penetrate easily in peoples' minds through emotional routes because there is less resistance. Telling a beautiful or a tragic story makes people feel sensitive to it and willing to participate in whatever subsequent event it might be. Critical thinking, on the contrary, is a dense environment for any ideas because people think, confront, research, and analyze. They don't just take the information as is. They are rational and factual. If there is no evidence of what they are told, they reject the idea and the arguments altogether.

The use of emotions in advertising is obvious. The tagline "Love is what makes a Subaru a Subaru" might easily penetrate the minds of those who are emotional about cars, while factual people will ignore the tagline and focus on the car's features: "What has love to do with cars?"

All campaigns for animals' adoption show them in a pitiful state, along with an actors' dramatic tone of voice with a depressing background music narrating their story so that people get emotional and are willing to donate money to save them and be rewarded with a plush and a T-shirt.

Just like nature, people tend to take the shortest and easiest paths. They make decisions based on little and incomplete information. In nature, this explains mirages and optical illusions. We see what our minds create for us based on very little information. Our brain tells stories we want to believe in. When you take shortcuts rather than examining the information, you are getting emotionally involved and sometimes experiencing an illusion. If that was not true, how could Coca-Cola Company sell their Starlight-flavored Coke? And how could Kroger find consumers for their Unicorn-flavored cookies?

These are all the ideas that ignited the willingness to write a book that would explain tribes and communities through the stories of humankind. This book is an invitation to see and accept people just as they are: as people. It breaks away from the labelization of individuals based on race, sex, and gender. People are much more than that: they are vectors as well as outcomes of cultures and this is what makes them interesting. The fascinating multicultural realm has so much to offer to those who want to go beyond physical traits to know more about people other than what is only apparent.

Thereby, this book addresses all those who are curious and fascinated by intercultural relationships. Businesspeople, academics, marketing professionals, and students alike will benefit from the deeper understanding of multiculturalism this book provides, as will anyone else willing to improve their multicultural skills. It tells the fascinating story of multicultural marketing and how vital and overlooked it is by companies. Since the beginning of the reading, the book will take you through the different eras of our existence and development as human beings to the unique reality of multiculturalism. From the stories told in tribes around the fire place to the current stories posted and shared in virtual communities, this book reinforces some myths while clarifying some others. It explains that consumers are more reactive to the stories told about companies and brands than to their products.

Page after page, the reader sees the story of humankind and of multiculturalism unfold and be explained through the lenses of science and storytelling. Our aim is to promote multiculturalism and all the benefits it provides to those who appreciate it. In an era when words are used instinctively and often inaccurately, it is important to get back to fundamental definitions prior to trying to understand the power of multiculturalism. When a word is used all the time in all situations like "culture" has been, it loses its meaning and becomes a simple incantation. Let's not forget that storytelling is the use of words that can make an impact on listeners. Such words are carefully selected by marketers to maximize impact on their consumers.

We demonstrate, here, that we have always been multicultural but that today we get confused and don't know how to handle multiculturalism. We are influenced by the feeling of globalization, of a unified stream of thoughts and conceptual inaccuracy created and sustained by the use of inappropriate vocabulary.

This book is the first one in the multicultural marketing field. Its unique approach bringing together science, marketing, and storytelling is thoroughly illustrated with real-life examples and first-hand experience. The ideas, theories, and statements presented in this book will perhaps challenge some of your deepest beliefs or they might as well comfort you in your own opinions. Ultimately, this book is an invitation to reflection, to critical thinking, to objectivity and to the liberty of accepting what is different.

Other books with similar titles speak about minorities and give it a quantitative approach to multiculturalism. We don't agree. Culture is not about quantity. Culture is qualitative because every single person representing a given culture counts. We also don't take a majority/minority approach to culture. We find it demeaning because in culture there is no major and minor, there is no superior or inferior; there is only different and we understand those differences as being positive. What's more, this is a relative concept because minorities in a country are majorities in other countries. All cultures have the same weight in multiculturalism and deserve the same respect. Culture is not about size or volume; it is about values.

In addition, other books on similar topics classify cultures as Asian, African, Hispanic, Caucasian, and so on, as if they were a whole homogenous lot. We, on the other hand, explain the reasons why this is an inaccurate way of defining cultures by digging deep into the roots of humankind and the emergence of cultures, all based on scientific discoveries. We go far beyond what can be found in blogs or in the popular mainstream publications. In this book, we explore and explain cultures and set multinational marketing apart from multicultural marketing, terms which are often used indistinctively.

This introduction lays out the foundations of the cultural complexities that we will study in this book. Unlike multinational marketing, multicultural marketing studies these same cultural idiosyncrasies within the same country, most of them being created by the power of storytelling.

This book is constituted of eight chapters. Each chapter starts with a brief overview named "What's the story?" and finishes with the implications for multicultural marketing and the key takeaways to help with understanding and designing better multicultural marketing strategies.

Chapter 1 defines culture and cultural stereotypes to clearly explain the differences between what is innate and what is learned. In this chapter, the differences between culture and community are made clear. The role of emotions in creating stories and the perception of reality are presented in order to lay down the ground to the understanding of multiculturalism and the role of storytelling in creating both real and virtual communities.

Chapter 2 describes the beginning of storytelling by taking us back to the Stone Age, when people would gather around the fire and tell fantastic or glorious stories to the rest of the tribe. Those stories were passed on from one generation to the next, sometimes with add-ons and some other times with slightly different interpretations. It is important to go back to the basics of storytelling before we understand its role in a multicultural world. Because we all belong to the same species, all cultures can relate to the origins of storytelling.

In *Chapter 3*, we travel back in time to reconnect with our deepest roots as a species. Taking children as the most natural storytellers makes it easier to understand where we come from and why we change with adulthood. Playing is part of everyone's life; however, the games change with aging and with the times the world goes through. The role of myths as well as the influence of media is described as drivers of human behavior.

Chapter 4 stresses the power of our brains in guiding our behaviors and how much they can be influenced by external stimuli and lead us to either make rushed and short-term survival decisions or plan on the long run. All our needs, aims, and expectations in life rest on one of the three main parts of our brains which are responsible for our answers to any situation. We might thus react instinctively, rationally, or emotionally to external events.

In *Chapter 5*, emotions and rationality are explained as factors influencing peoples' perception of reality and their ability to learn and understand their surroundings. Science explains most of our reactions to reality and leads to defining different levels of intelligence, namely emotional intelligence (EI) and cultural intelligence (CQ). The scientific approach to this chapter sheds light on multiculturalism and multiracialism and questions the use of technology in helping peoples from different cultures to live together.

Chapter 6 explains the existence and the power of communities. Brand communities and online communities are what marketers are creating and working with today, although communities have always existed and they were called tribes. Brands become myths and consequently create communities thanks to the stories told about them and about their founders. Such stories are fascinating to people who aspire to be as successful as them and take them as role models. Often, brand loyalty comes from the admiration of the founder or of the CEO.

Chapter 7 introduces the concept of openness to diversity as a measure of multiculturalism and presents intriguing research findings on the topic. It also argues that globalization is the opposite of multiculturalism and that technology is intensifying the feeling of a unified world culture. Finally, the role of flags for national and cultural representations are presented as storytellers of the deep-rooted history and values of nations as opposed to flags used to represent communities that are based on common interests rather than on cultures.

Chapter 8 guides your steps in designing a multicultural marketing strategy. It goes over the main cultural orientations created by authors highly specialized in intercultural studies and explains the use of mainstream frameworks for cultural analysis. It then introduces the cultural analysis grid to help understand the cultures targeted by the company.

It follows the specificities of a multicultural marketing strategy, which is finalized with the multicultural marketing plan.

In *Conclusion* of the book, we highlight the importance of multiculturalism and the role played by multicultural marketing in helping people to get to know different cultures and enjoy all the benefits and richness it brings to their lives through storytelling.

Enjoy the stories!

CHAPTER 1

Biology, Culture, and Archetypes

What's the Story?

Once upon a time, race and ethnicity were used as synonyms. It was important to define and explain both concepts and present cultural archetypes and emotions (transmitted by stories) as the engines that trigger interest and engagement from consumers. We introduce the concept of ethnocentrism and its fundamental role in accepting or rejecting foreign brands and people according to the subjective perception of reality and stereotypes.

There has been considerable confusion between terms that have been assimilated to each other in the popular language, but are fundamentally different in their definitions and quite independent of one another. Although this might look like something without concerning consequences, it remains a misleading practice.

Terms such as race and ethnicity have been used indistinctively, while they are totally different and independent of each other. Biological schemata are universal and common to all humans, but the forces adopted by a given culture for survival are cultural archetypes (Rapaille, 2007). They organize not only myth, religion, art, architecture, and so on, but also basic rituals such as eating habits and dress codes. They are all different and specific to each culture, not to each race.

When a company such as Gap ventures abroad, they change the sizes of their clothes because consumers are physically different: taller and skinnier, with different body curves—what is very important in multinational marketing, otherwise their international consumers won't be able to wear their products. The company makes less effort in multicultural marketing assuming that all consumers are alike in their domestic market. Yet, Gap consumers in the United States resemble those from several countries the company adapts their products to. That is why some people buy online from other countries and from other companies where they find better fit for their bodies.

Cultural archetypes are the laws of the culture in which we are born that pertain to human relationships and human organizations. They are part of a culture's condition, conscious and unconscious, and represent the degree to which people recognize and live in harmony with such basic concepts as freedom and prohibition, equal opportunity and unequal wealth, individualism and uniformity, and fairness and violence (Rapaille 2007).

Archetypology is the study of relationships. It studies the relationship among the forces of a culture and the system or structure that organizes these forces into the field of tensions necessary for the culture to survive. The biological need for survival is the central element of culture. If cultures don't successfully address this need, they will disappear. Archetypes transcend the empirical world of time and place, organize basic rituals, and create an image that amplifies and depersonalizes because it resonates with collective unconscious.

Each culture not only perceives the world differently, but also articulates and organizes the world differently. Archetypes are what we assimilate when we learn a culture—a set of forms or practices that the culture deposits in those who belong to the same cultural system. Culture is form, not substance. It is not the result of individual behavior, but rather it is made possible by a collective social system of active forces that individuals have assimilated. Therefore, culture is a system of forces that includes norms and rules of language, collective representation of society, and the mechanism of a physical economy. Put in other words, culture is what enables us to live together.

There Are No Cultural Chromosomes

One of the most current confusions involves culture and race. Yet the difference is clear: race is biological while culture is social. Race is innate whereas culture is learned. While cultures tend to be country specific, race is boundaryless and spans across countries.

Let's take a story as an example. In the *Jungle Book*, Mowgli was a human being but was raised by wolves and behaved like one of them. He was biologically human, but his culture was the wolves' culture. Tarzan was human too, but was raised by monkeys and behaved like them. His culture was the monkeys' culture. This means, your biological background doesn't shape your mindset and behavior; your culture does it. And your culture is independent of your race; it has to do with who you are raised by and where.

You absorb the culture you were socialized in. The socialization process takes place when a child learns to live in a given culture, usually the culture they are raised in. And your brain will be shaped by that culture. As a consequence, you comply with the rules and accepted behavior of that specific culture.

When your parents migrate to a foreign country, you become bicultural because you learn, simultaneously, their culture and the culture you live in. Your parents will socialize you with their home culture, but school will socialize you with your host culture. As an adult, you will be able to navigate between the two cultures, knowing that practices, including language, are different at the workplace and at home. When your parents tell you stories about their home culture, they convey their feelings and emotions which are frequently based on nostalgia. Often, their narrative is positive about the country they left behind for some reason. This is how you grow up idealizing your parents' culture of origin and might, at some stage of your life, envisage migrating back to that country in order to reconnect with your deepest cultural roots.

Emotions Tell Us What Is of Value. They Guide Us, Letting Us Know Who We Ought to Be and What We Should Go After

Emotions are active, embodied responses to people, places, and events encountered in the world. Emotions are stronger than intellect; otherwise, why would people cry when their sports team loses a game? What does this ephemeral joy or sadness change in their daily lives? They will still have the same job, same home, and same salary whether the team wins or loses. When their team wins, the players surely earn more money, but the supporters don't. Their lives keep being exactly the same, unless they bet on one of the teams. Yet, this ephemeral satisfaction they experience virtually through the players seems to be a big deal to them. It is a collective phenomenon which would be pointless if it was just an individual experience. When people gather to speak about sports, they are telling stories about players, past and upcoming games.

As stated by the American memoirist Maya Angelou, "people will forget what you said, people will forget what you did, but people will never forget how you made them feel." We like people and stories that make us feel good. Positive emotions are memorized as are negative emotions, but we avoid the latter because they are painful and we look for stories that make us feel good.

If emotions are what move people to enjoy sports, they also help people to choose products. It goes from functional needs to the pleasure of possession. But emotions are temporal as is the pleasure of consumption. That is why we renew it often. Products, brands, and logos tell stories to consumers as does advertising and this is how people are enticed to buy the "right brand." As consumption is a social activity, people turn to social media in search of approval and validation of their personal decisions. Often, because they feel unable to make a decision, they leave it to influencers to decide for them so that they are reassured of making the "right choice."

Thanks to technology, we live in the "now" culture. Indeed, in a world of immediacy, nothing is built to last with the risk that what goes up very quickly goes down faster. Watching videos of people dancing or of funny cats and puppies leads to a very short emotional state. Dramas described in a few minutes on social media have the same effect. People are immediately in support or rejection of what they see on social media and, without taking the time to fact-check, they just share the emotion they are feeling at that very moment. Humans constantly make decisions based on impulses, gut feelings, or force of habit. Such decisions evade rational analysis. One simple cue is enough to accept or reject. This is how emotions take people from misery to ecstasy, and conversely in a few minutes.

We use emotions to create and categorize memories. And by the use of stories, we live in an illusionary reality created by storytelling. We create reality in our brains and we see what we expect to see and hear what we expect to hear. Companies no longer sell products; they sell experiences. These experiences stir emotions and generate memories. They embrace dramatic actions, sensory engagement, and temporal interaction. During the experience, customers create meanings and associations that become more important than the product itself.

When experiencing products, consumers go through an emotional journey. The experience has highs and lows, just like a story, because the relationship consumers have with products evolves overtime. Energy rises and falls depending on curiosity, pleasure, satisfaction, and external approval. Because emotions are so fundamental in peoples' lives, consumers don't shop anymore; they "experience" an interaction with products. Shopping yielded to shopping experience which leads to consumer experience and this is where customer satisfaction comes from. When you are an expatriate and live abroad, brands carry even more emotions and you will always pick the ones you are familiar with. Brand familiarity leads to trust (Karsaklian 2012).

Romanticism tells us that, in order to make the most of our human potential, we must have as many different experiences as we can. In marketing, it is all about experience: customer experience, shopping experience, travel experience, and so forth. We believe that those experiences make us a better person in helping us to enjoy life and create memorable experiences. In reality, we are so bored with our daily routines and comfort that anything a bit different sounds like a great experience to us. People pay high prices to spend a weekend in a place with no electricity and no wifi, but are in total panic when there is a power outage at home. Consumption is meant to widen our horizons, fulfill our human potential, and make us happier by satisfying our physical, psychological, and social needs.

When it comes to multicultural marketing, consumption widens our horizons because it turns into multicultural consumption. The pleasure comes from being offered products that fit perfectly in our culture, but it also comes from the opportunity of sampling products from other cultures without leaving our city or country. This is the argument of restaurants offering foods from other cultures, concerts with rhythms from abroad, as well as movies and games from all different cultures.

Emotions also explain the growth of the pet care market. The love people have for their pets is what makes them spend around U.S.$210 billion worldwide in premium food, grooming, and toys. The market is expected to continue to grow at a rate of 5.6 percent, reaching sales of over U.S.$300 billion by 2028. Their pets are members of their family and their owners are called pet moms and pet dads. These figures prompt the following question: if humans can convey so much love to animals from other species, why can't they do the same with animals from their own species? Why would they reject humans that look different or speak differently?

Sapiens are supposed to be the only intelligent animal, but their greed makes them the cruelest too. Not happy of having already exterminated the Neanderthals, *sapiens* are exterminating wild animals for money. Abundant species in the past are becoming rare today: rhinoceros, elephants, tigers, and so on. Other animals might kill to eat and fight for territory but they don't try to exterminate other species. They cope with them in the jungle. And humans are unable to live with other humans on the same planet. It does not make any sense.

Reality Is a Cultural Perception

Life is movement because time is an organizer of activities. But the use of time is culture specific. Each culture decides on how to use the three elements of movement: time, space, and energy. The opposite of movement is death. Yet, the definition of culture evolved from the religious belief that the end of life was decided by Gods to the scientific definition of the body's technical failure.

Cultures evolve just like our lives evolve throughout time; we learn, we experience, we convey, we change. Put in other words, life is going forth whereas death is returning home, to our roots.

As we experience our daily lives, every external factor or living being has an impact on our routines: plants, pets, and people. Any new factor can provide our lives with more balance or more imbalance. Our whole lives, we seek out for balance so that we are psychologically stable. Life is balancing constraints and pleasure in a livable way. It is hard work to stay alive and to socialize and that is why most people don't want to leave their zones of comfort. Staying among people similar to them is so much easier. Is it worth going through the trouble of understanding other people's culture just to expand our personal network? Most people think it is not. And that is evidenced when we measure openness to diversity. Most people are not open to people different from them, although social desirability states the opposite.

Cultural forces are balanced because they come in pairs. This balance gives a culture the illusion of immobility or of permanence, when in fact these forces are dynamic and usually pulling in opposite directions. It can be perceived, by outsiders, as paradoxical forces or contradictions, when they are actually two sides of the same coin. We live in a world of duality.

Often people ask who is right and who is wrong in a story. What are the easiest cultures to work with? The first question has to do with ethnocentrism. Everyone is ethnocentric, that is, we think that our culture is the right one, what is perfectly normal, because this is where we feel more comfortable Karsaklian (2014). The more ethnocentric people are, the less open to other cultures they are, because they are persuaded that their culture is the best one. They don't see the point in learning about other cultures.

Cultural ethnocentrism also applies to the choices made by consumers. The more ethnocentric they are, the less likely they are to buy foreign brands. International marketing theories have identified the country of origin effect as a factor of acceptance or rejection of foreign brands (Herz and Diamantopoulos 2017). Some brands were respected because of the recognized deep-rooted expertise of specific countries in producing specific products: food from France, cars from Germany, technology from Japan, fashion from Italy, beauty products from South Korea, and entertainment from the United States, just to name a few. The brands told stories about these countries which were known for being the best ones because of their history in mastering the needed quality for their products in those specific industries.

The country of origin effect can have either a positive or a negative impact on consumers. For instance, consumers might boycott some brands because they come from a country having issue with the country they live in, while purchasing other brands from the same country without knowing their country of origin! This happens because they don't go beyond what "they were told." Yet, a quick online research can elucidate the origin of a brand. That is why some brands use their nationality as an argument to sell their products when it is favorable while others, fearing rejection, hide their country of origin. Consumers also seem to be unable to separate politics from business. Has the conflict between countries been generated by those companies or have them just been caught up in the middle of a diplomatic crisis created by their governments? So many times, in those situations, the backlash is on the consumer rather than on the companies that were rejected because consumers are unable to purchase their favorite brands, while the companies have other markets to tap into.

The second question is culture relative. Put in other words, whether some cultures are easier or harder to deal with depends on the cultural distance Karsaklian (2020). Cultural distance measures the differences and similarities among cultures. The closer your culture is to another one, the smaller the cultural distance and the higher the likelihood of you feeling comfortable with that culture. This is based on similarities and differences in their cultural traits. Note that cultural distance has nothing to do with geographical distance. It is not because there is a physical closeness that cultures are similar. This statement opposes the widespread habit of defining cultures geographically: Europeans, Asians, Africans, Latin Americans, and so on. France and Germany share a border, but couldn't be more culturally different. The same applies to the United States and Mexico, or Argentina and Brazil.

Today, we witness a shift from the country of origin effect toward supporting social causes as a factor influencing purchases. We went from factual and tangible quality evidence to emotional and personal criteria for decision making. Companies display their belonging to communities: woman-owned company, black owned, LGBTQ+ friendly, and so on. It is a whole different story told to consumers aiming at enticing them to buy their products as a way of supporting a fair cause. Consumers believe that, in doing so, they fight discrimination by supporting communities that have been discriminated centuries ago. When customers' choices are based on quality, competition is fair because the best product wins. But when the choices are based on emotional ties to persons, all those who don't belong to those communities, because they were not born with those physical traits, are discriminated and lose sales even if their products were better. Objectivity yields to subjectivity.

This takes us to the power of perception; we tend to see what we are looking for. It makes everything easier to bring different people to a common denominator without minding cultural differences among those people. It is a mistake because this is how people and businesses get surprised with their failures in multicultural settings. Perception is active and temporal and our working memory can hold on to only a few objects at a time. This is how cultural stereotypes are very useful. They narrow down a whole population to few cultural traits so that they are easier to memorize. Although they are not false, cultural stereotypes should be seen as an invitation to know more about that specific culture. Different cultures relate to and perceive things differently. Yet cultural stereotypes are often portrayed in TV shows and movies aiming at having the local population mocking those who live abroad with different mindsets and lifestyles without realizing that the same cultural communities live in their country too, what makes it multicultural.

What Is Culture After All?

Culture is a system of crystallized answers to biological needs (Rapaille 2007). If a culture succeeds in addressing these survival needs in a satisfactory way, the species will survive and the culture will with it. Just like trees, we have deep roots, need to feel grounded, but want to branch out. Cultural identity implies being grounded in a culture. That is why when Burlington's slogan states that low prices and customer care are their culture, they are speaking about their positioning which has nothing to do with culture. No wonder people get confused with the concept of culture as it is used inaccurately everywhere. The word "culture" has become trendy and everyone is mistakenly using it without really knowing what they are talking about. The issue is that they lead a whole population toward inaccuracy and cultural ignorance.

Rapaille (2007) defines cultural madness as wanting to treat all cultures equally, when it is more respectful to accept their fundamental differences. He states that when it comes to improvement, for instance, in some cultures it is seen as a continuous process, whereas in other cultures, improvement is only considered when there is urgency in solving a problem. Indeed, universalism is a myth and myths vanish once people stop believing in them. All the people who have been facing multicultural difficulties know that.

The globalization of the economy does not have to be at the cost of the disappearance of individual cultures. There is diversity of cultures in the global economy. Why do people get homesick in a globalized world? Because cultures are different and it requires effort to adjust to new habits and practices. People get homesick when they miss the comfort of undertaking normal mental highways. After a while people, mainly expatriates, grow tired of having to decode everything locals say and do. This is called cultural fatigue (Karsaklian 2019).

When we aim at equality, we believe in something unreal. Humans are all genetically different and we evolve, generation after generation, by being exposed to different environmental influences. Thus, we develop different qualities leading to different places in our societies. We might want to be equal in front of the law, but there is nothing intrinsically universal in human beings. The laws of physics will keep the universe stable independently of human actions. These are universal laws. Human laws and rules are based on beliefs which can collapse at any moment if people just realize that they are the fruit of peoples' imagination that made you believe that they were real. That is why laws change all the time. Depending on the president or the political party, laws are changed according to each one's beliefs (or goals) and imposed on the whole population by making them believe that they are done on their behalf and for their good; laws are there to protect us, that is the story we are told.

Why Be Different If You Can Be Like Everyone Else?

An archetypal user of a product is called persona and companies expect their consumers to identify with that persona. It portrays a specific demographic, culture, and lifestyle. But in a multicultural world, the persona needs to be able to incorporate several different cultures to ensure cultural inclusion. Consumers unable to identify with the persona created by the brand reject that brand. Every persona has a personality as does every brand. If they don't match with consumers' personality, if consumers don't see themselves in that brand, they won't experience it. This difficulty might explain the rapid growth of the use of digital humans, which are largely used by companies as digital influencers with a personality and followers. If people can believe in such a contradictory story (human and digital), they can believe in anything.

The relationship consumers have with products goes through three stages: visceral, as an immediate reaction to colors, form, brand name, and logo; behavioral, action undertaken such as purchase or rejection; and reflective memories and associations such as satisfaction/dissatisfaction. Thus, the rule of three applies to consumer behavior. As a matter of fact, most of our lives turn around three options: the three main takeaways, the three tips to succeed, the three things to avoid when working with another culture, the first three things to do, and the three adjectives we use to illustrate a statement. In marketing, we often measure the three "top of mind" brand names and the top tier of more valuable brands.

There are often three options to everything we say or are offered with, otherwise it feels like there is no closure—something is missing. When trying to solve a problem, we often look at three plausible scenarios. Sometimes what we prefer might or might not be probable, plausible, or possible or applicable to different cultures. Yet, we need to have the options, to ensure that if our favorite one doesn't work, we still have two others to back us up. The lack of a third option implies the feeling of lack of closure, which generates discomfort. We were conditioned to expect the third option, which creates the expectation of something that should happen but when it does not happen it makes people uncomfortable.

Some companies are giving the same kind of choice to their consumers so that they can customize the products as they like. The choice of shapes and colors for the product, packaging, and logos is critical because they all carry emotions. But colors have different meanings in different cultures, and companies need to be mindful of those differences when deciding on their target markets. Thus companies such as Nike offer a limited choice of colors to customize their shoes and these colors are chosen differently by consumers from different cultures. People want to be different but not too different to avoid rejection. They need to fit in their cultural communities.

Some people are more adventurous being categorized as growth mindsets. They enjoy challenges, change, and novelty. Some others feel more comfortable with routines and are the so-called fixed minds.

They don't like new challenges because they avoid the unforgettable feeling of not being good at something. In their minds, talents are fixed and there is no point in trying to learn new skills. They enjoy their comfort zone. They would rather follow than lead; rather agree than analyze. They won't give much thought to what they do. Their only goal is to fit in. They will thus be against what everyone else is against, without even questioning the validity of the cause. They will wear the same brands as others to be part of that brand community as their main fear is to be singled out. And they will stick to stereotypes if this is what everyone else is doing, without even wondering what is beyond those stereotypes.

Implications for Multicultural Marketing

Humans don't perceive stories just like distant narratives. We live on stories and we are part of them. The more fantastic our stories, the more connections and followers we have. We are impressed by characters and want to impress others by playing the role of main characters of many stories that fill our lives with joy, sadness, surprise, depression, and love.

The understanding of the fundamental differences between race and culture is critical to be successful in multicultural marketing. Race relates to biological needs while culture relates to social needs. Some companies are more successful abroad than in their domestic markets due to several factors, one of them being cultural adaptation abroad while neglecting similar cultural differences in their domestic markets.

Key Takeaways From Chapter 1

- Multinational companies should benefit from synergies between their multinational and multicultural marketing strategies. They both can serve each other.
- Companies should not overlook cultural differences within one same market.
- Companies that neglect subcultures miss part of the market share due to insufficient cultural adaptation of their products.

CHAPTER 2

We Create a Story World to Live Inside

What's the Story?

Once upon a time, people liked to share private information on social platforms and thought that real and virtual lives were the same. They would drown in stories of all sorts including those called "reality shows" or any other entertainment product such as TV series, movies, and videogames. Because the brain can't tell the difference between reality and fiction, they became intertwined in consumers' minds. This has to do with communication, which is essential to survival: it was so in the Stone Age, it is still so today.

Our lives are a sequence of stories without which our existence is meaningless. We exist through stories about us. We write memories because we already know the end of our stories: we will die. We don't know how, when, and where, but we know it will happen. One of the few certainties we have in life is that it expires. Our life is a grand narrative and social media became the vehicle whereby we share our stories. People document their lives with videos and photos which they share with people they will never get to know. Whether they are dancing, playing with their children and pets, working out, traveling, or getting together with family and friends, they are writing the story of their lives and sharing them in real time.

Tattoos are also a way of leaving proofs of the different phases and events of peoples' lives, but on their skins. Tattoos tell a story about those who carry them. Sometimes they get obsolete, because life has changed and some of the drawings are no longer appropriate. It is time to tell a different story. Rap as a music style fulfills the same mission. There is music but the rhythm is a narrative, where the singer speaks rather than sings along with the notes in a narrative of life situations, questions about society and politics, often with a rebellious flavor.

We endeavor to understand our lives as a grand narrative, reconstructing the past (as we were told by our families) and imagining the future in such a way as to provide it with some purpose, unity, and meaning. This means that all that we know about our past comes from our family's interpretation and a few pictures (Karsaklian 2016). Thus, an uncle was a great person, but that cousin was nasty. How can you know how great and how nasty they were? In all families, there were the nice victims of the nasty heartless others. That is the story you are told and you believe it because you were not there to know what really happened. Also, why would your family lie to you?

This is just like what we are told in the news. Sometimes not even the journalists were there; they just picked up the information from other sources and told their story as if it was the absolute truth with no interpretations. People believe it because it was in the news and share those stories as facts. But stories are not facts, they are interpretations. After a while, the interpretation turns into "the truth" because this is the only version of the story going around. And because of immediacy, less and less people fact-check and analyze the information. They just pass it on.

The mistakes we make about the human world and how to live in it are built in us and influence our perception of reality. The brain defends our flawed model of the world with several biases. When we come across any new input, we immediately judge it. If it's consistent with our model of reality, our brain gives a subconscious feeling of yes. If it is not, the answer is no. These emotional responses happen before we go through any process of conscious reasoning. The rational response when encountering someone with alien ideas would be to attempt to understand them, but the emotional response would be to reject the idea and the person altogether.

Our brain treats threats to our neural models the same way as it protects our bodies from physical attacks putting us into a fight mode. In order to not be hurt, we tend to avoid people with different ideas and backgrounds from ours. Everyone thinks they are right. Even when doing wrong, we find ourselves justifying our actions as self-defense against a provocation or a threat, which can be only on our minds.

Several multinational companies experience rejection when they first arrive in a foreign country. This can be caused by cultural stereotypes but also by the stories the foreign consumers are told about the company. McDonald's went through severe rejection when the company first settled in France. At that time, there were no threatening competitors to McDonald's on the French market and the company thought that it would be easy to introduce their standardized concept to that juicy market. It was not. French consumers rejected the American imperialism of McDonald's and its fast food concept altogether. There were countrywide boycotts and the company needed to review their whole communication campaign. To tone down such rejection, the story they told was that McDonald's might have been born in the United States, but was a French company working with local suppliers to satisfy French consumers' needs. It helped, but it was not enough; things only became better once the company adapted to the local culture by introducing salads, water, yogurt, fresh fruits, and beer!

From the multicultural standpoint, ever since the company moved their headquarters back in Chicago, they have been offering worldwide menus to local consumers. This way, the company shows how multinational and multicultural they are.

The Positive Moral Self-Image

Ironically, the people who rationalize our existence, stating that life is limited in time, that we will all eventually die, and that everything we build is ephemeral, are treated as sick, depressive, and mentally ill people. Yet, everyone knows that it is true and real. Denial doesn't remove what is real. Every story comes to an end.

For the rest of us, we avoid this topic. We live our lives as if we were eternal. The search for longevity or even immortality has always been a challenge to humans. People are willing to pay big amounts of money to look and feel younger as if this would make them live longer and better. People live longer today thanks to scientific progress. But they do not always live well. Science has extended peoples' lives but we don't know how to look after our elders yet. From this point of view, cultures that believe in life after death have a smoother understanding and less traumatic perception of the end of life.

And we are scared at the future because we are scared at the unknown. We might feel very strong today but we don't know what will happen to us tomorrow. And what if there is no longer a mob to follow and we need to think and make our way alone? How are we going to speak to real people after having spent most of our lives in a virtual world? How to live in a world where we need to know more about our neighbors than about the celebrities we admire?

We live on stories: the news, posts on social media, testimonies, gossip, lawsuits between famous people, movies, TV shows, success stories, and dramas. The more fantastic the story, the more people are fascinated by them. The more heroes are created, the more people are inspired by them. But these stories are just stories. They are interpretations of facts or totally made up stories, just like most "reality" shows and TV series. It makes storytellers' job so much easier because no one looks for the factual truth.

What makes a nation are the stories told about it. And so are cultures created and sustained across generations. We have been wired to believe and enjoy stories. In doing so, our brain creates a world for us to live in and populates it with good and bad people and makes us the main character of the story. This is how we turn into a star overnight and become the center of all attention. This is also why social media is so popular: it has the power of making anyone become a star. People have a platform where they tell stories about themselves and turn into celebrities thanks to likers and followers. Most posts are contentless, because most of them are about people talking about themselves, their pets, their children, their job search, their graduations, their frustrations, and so on. In a world where content yields to figures, all that counts is the number of followers, likes, shares, and comments.

And in this virtual world, anyone offering a different version of a tale, even based on facts, is rejected and marginalized. People reject everything that doesn't suit the beliefs created by the stories in their minds. It is people, not events, that attract attention. That is how celebrities are created and why reality TV is so successful. There is no plot in these shows; only people living their "normal lives" so that the audience feels like being part of them from the inside. It is not a brain challenge to understand their stories, because they are so easy to relate to.

Drama triggers multiple emotions: pity, fear, sadness, and sometimes relief and even happiness when there is a happy ending to it. Contemporary stories seem to have found the emotion that attracts people the most: fear. Stories are more fantastic (*Walking Dead, Stranger Next Door*), more fictitious (*Transformers, Avengers*), more dramatic (*Kardashians, All Star Shore*), and more violent (*Killing Eve, Snow Piercer*). These are just a few examples in a multitude of TV shows and movies people enjoy watching because there is more action than content.

In one course assignment, my students were required to conduct a market research about TV shows, because those are products just like any other services. They were free to choose any TV show from any style and from any country. Their findings clearly demonstrated that interest and loyalty to the shows increased as the level of violence increased and there was "more blood." In spite of the alarming outcomes of this market research, it is easy to understand that contemporary audiences are lured to drama and violence rather than to comedy or romance. A quick comparison between TV shows from the 1960s to 1990s and those of today highlights the big gap in the standards and the definition of "entertainment." Shows such as *I Dream of Jeannie, Bewitched, Father Knows Best, The Golden Girls, Married with Children, and Everybody Loves Raymond*, just to name a few, portrayed families, friendship, and love in a very colorful and bright décor, as opposed to today's shows which are darker and focused on revenge, fight, torture, and murder. These shows are broadcast at the same time slots as the previous ones, meaning that they are made available to all audiences, including children.

Batman with Adam West and Burt Ward in the 1960s was colorful and portrayed the two heroes fighting the bad guys. Today, Batman is dark and sometimes evil, and fights Captain America, while both were supposed to be heroes on the good guys' side. We can thus assume that the taste for storytelling has changed. The feel-good emotion brought by old stories seems to be reached by fear now. This kind of emotion, seen as universal by the production companies, enables them to export these shows around the world.

We Experience Pressure Every Day

Brains are on constant alert to understand the environment and control it. Everything our attention rests upon triggers a sensation, preceding conscious thought. Human worlds are haunted with minds, faces, and memories. When we look at anything, we see it with our past. Sense-making is the association between what we see and our own personal histories because there should be an association with what we know and believe to make sense. We need to create a context to fit the story in so that it can make sense to us.

Our minds understand cause–effect relationships. When we don't know the cause, we assume or create one to propagate and direct others' minds in the direction we chose. As the cause has already been given to others exposed to your "information," they take it as truth and their minds don't need to look for the real causes or check the accuracy of the ones you state.

Without critical thinking, people just go with the flow without really knowing what they are doing. It is as if their brain was split with no connections between both hemispheres. They receive "an order" and mechanically follow it. Thus, in their neural realm, they make up a cause–effect story to explain what they are doing but they don't actually know the cause.

Even with critical thinking, we rarely know why we do what we do and how we feel. We confabulate and more often than not try to guess than really know. There are so many factors that contribute to our behavior and we are not always aware of them or of all of them. We might not be very good at introspection either or want to avoid giving too much thought to what can turn out, making us feel uncomfortable if we dig too deep. We are not in complete control of ourselves.

That is why life is a real struggle and we have regrets. We are disappointed in ourselves because we are unable to explain some of our actions. Sometimes we do things that don't sound or look like us. We are as surprised as people who witness our actions. These are stories we don't like to tell.

It is impressive how many times a day we boycott ourselves even when we want to believe that we have a rational explanation to what we do.

We discover who we are every day and often because other people confront us asking for explanations. This is when avoidance and denial come into play. We don't want to answer because we don't know how to answer. Admitting it to others will make us look silly and without control of our own lives and actions. For example, it makes it much easier to say that we buy products to support a cause (even if it is not ours, but it is the trend), than that we are scared at being rejected if we don't do so.

Sometimes we are proud of ourselves and some other times we are disappointed. "I can't believe these words are coming out of my mouth." "I can't believe I did that." We are in internal conflict and what we say contradicts what we do and sometimes what we think. We manifest two different versions of ourselves at once. We can desire something at the conscious level and yet subconsciously need something entirely different. We are multiple and confabulatory, skating on the thin ice of sanity. We are a battleground for the invisible forces of our own subconscious minds. "I knew it was wrong, but did it anyway."

The emotions we experience when under the power of story don't happen by accident. Humans have evolved to respond in certain ways to tales of heroism and villainy linked to our survival. In this era of information, we might pride ourselves for our technology and speed of our brains, but as humans, we are still in the Stone Age. We are still moved by primal forces because we still have the same needs and fears (Harari 2015).

Back to the Stone Age

Communication and cooperation were key to surviving in tribes of 150 or more people, although there were clusters by family. In order to be functional, it was essential that they cooperated, putting the collective needs before their own. They survived for tens of thousands of years because they managed to do so. They were able to control self-interested behaviors without the help of police or judiciary or even any written law. The way to prevent it was storytelling. When the story involved praised behavior, those people were celebrated. But when they were described as being self-interested and selfish, they would be attacked, punished, and banished, which would put their survival in jeopardy. This is how stories kept the tribes together as a functional and cooperating unit (Harari 2015).

Today, we pile up laws, norms, rules, and sanctions but self-interests take precedence over the general interests. In some collective cultures, the communitarian aspect is stronger than in more individualistic cultures; that is, the group still takes precedence over the individual. In more individualistic cultures, you should stand out and display accomplishment. Yet, individualistic cultures have been seeing communities create movements pro and against several tribes. It has been growing on Internet because they all ask people to join them without really explaining the benefits of their aims. More than once, people who donated time and money to causes that looked genuine and in the interest of their tribe (community) realized that they had been used to contribute to serve personal interests.

Humans have two major ambitions: to get along and get ahead. We are driven to connect and to dominate, which often triggers dishonesty, hypocrisy, and betrayal. Humans are interested in the status of themselves and others at an almost obsessional degree. They pursue status with ferocity. Their subjective well-being, self-esteem, and mental and physical health appear to depend on the level of status they are accorded to by others. Everyone seems to feel unfairly lacking in status and most of them turn to social media looking for approval and validation.

There is nothing more likely to make a person mad than the removal of their status. When the reality of the external world finally becomes undeniable, people's internal model of it falls apart. The entire self collapses as does their theory of control and to successfully manipulate their environment. Counter-knowledge and denial only work when there is not enough external evidence. This is the mechanism of cancel culture. Exclusion is the highest punishment a human being can endure. Because we live in tribes, being shown as a traitor and being excluded is the utmost humiliation.

Psychologists define humiliation as the removal of any ability to claim status. Severe humiliation has been described as an annihilation of the self. It is toxic and explains most of the worst behaviors humans engage in. It assimilates to revenge. Oftentimes, it is indeed revenge from those who can't accept ideas and opinions different from theirs. Because they are unable to factually counter-argue or to debate, they just cancel the people who threaten their status and weaken their ability to control others' minds.

Humans are paradoxical: they riot for the freedom of speech at the same time as they practice censorship by shutting the mouths of those who don't tell the same story than them. Unfortunately, the more restrictions and prohibitions there are, the poorer minded people become. The more people use any kind of weapon, including words and riots, the more the state is in confusion. And the more laws and order are issued, the more robbery is encouraged, as rather than being seen as role models, the people who create those restrictions don't demonstrate consistency between what they preach and what they do. And this is why there is a lack of respect for others. In addition, circumventing laws and norms become a game and a challenge leading to celebrity. People record themselves when looting, raping, and killing and post them on Internet to become famous. Surprisingly, these videos are not always canceled by the online platforms and are presented as "information," rather than a reward for misconduct.

Stories are tribal propaganda (Storr 2020). They control their group; they manipulate their members into behaving in ways that benefit them. A human tribe can be viewed as a status game that all its members are playing, its rules being recorded in its stories. Our primitive cognition makes us think in tribal stories. Whenever the status of our tribe is threatened, we fire up. The sense of war is spread in the networks and people go to war against the threat. The brain enters this state of war because this is a threat to its theory of control. Enemies are always portrayed as ugly and selfish, while the heroes are humble and generous. Yet, history has shown that no sides of a war are totally innocent or totally guilty. We allow a simplistic narrative to deceive us because it is easier than facing the truth.

It is in the first two decades of our lives that we form ourselves out of our experience. It's when our models of reality are built. As adults, the hallucinations we experience as truth are built out of our pasts. We see, feel, and explain the world partly with our damage. Because damage happens when our models are still being built, the flaws it creates become incorporated into who we are. They're internalized. And parents convey their own frustrations to their children. There are generations who hate some cultures without even knowing them based exclusively on the stories told by their parents and grandparents about some past war, some punishment, and some humiliation. In these stories, their families' tribes were victims attacked by heartless opposing tribes. The same war told by people from both sides sounds like two different stories.

Humans are directed toward goals. We want things and we strive to get them. Goal direction is the foundational mechanism on top of which all our other urges are built: ambitions, love, disappointments, and betrayals. Humans have a compulsion to make things happen in their environment. It is our basic need. Our goals give our lives logic and order. They provide us with a reality around which we want the rest of the world to gravitate. Our perception organizes itself around this reality. What we see and feel at any moment depends on what we are trying to get at that moment. Later on, we might be proud or ashamed of the actions we undertook at that very moment, because that moment has passed and we are in a different context now. We might not even be a member of the same tribe anymore.

Escapism—The Virtual Life Is So Much Easier

Anyone can turn into Spiderman thanks to Meta Quest. Indeed, this device and software created by Meta (former Facebook) has been acquiring new customers thanks to several apps that "transport" people to wherever they would like to go and to be whatever they would like to be or they wish they were already. It is all illusionary, but it gives people more wings than Redbull! All you have to do is wear the headset as you would your glasses and you are already flying like a free bird without even leaving your bedroom. Some would say that turning into Spiderman gives the ultimate feeling of freedom.

One of these apps called RecRoom creates an informal environment where anyone can hang out either with their friends in a private room or in a public place with unfamiliar people, just like in a Starbucks. And unlike meeting through a computer's screen, it feels like everyone is there in person, while they are miles away from each other. They can chat, have drinks, and even play board games together. It saves time and the hassle of driving or commuting. Better yet, it enables people from different countries to hang out as if they were in the same place.

As fantastic, handy, and realistic it might seem to be, virtual reality prevents people from meeting real people and experiencing something memorable together. It remains an illusionary décor simulating real situations. It takes out most of the emotions needed to learn and remember an experience by providing the ability of switching from one "place" to another without spending enough time to dig deep into understanding foreign cultures.

This ultimate feeling of freedom is a bit of a paradox when you do everything from home: your food, devices, clothes, and cars are home delivered; you work remotely, build virtual networks, attend virtual events and courses, and play games online. The story told by freedom as opposed to captivity implies freedom of movement, which means being able to physically go wherever you want whenever you want. We were unhappy when we were locked down during the pandemic, but we keep going with the same routine several months after all restrictions have been lifted. We are animals of habit. This is one of the reasons why the term "freedom" has been used every day, everywhere by so many people and applied to so many situations that it is losing its core definition to become an incantation rather than a concept. Some stories told on behalf of freedom have nothing to do with being free.

This also highlights the fact that consumers are trainable. As much as they complained about the lockdowns, they keep behaving the same way now that they are free: remote working, online shopping, online gaming, home delivery, and so on, their alibi being "It is so handy and convenient," "It saves me time," "I don't have time to go shopping," and so on. People living and working in the same city meet remotely rather than in person to "avoid driving or commuting." This alibi is a story told by consumers to explain their behavior, which, they know, is a bit contradictory with what they often preach or claim. The gap between what people say and what people do is the same gap we find in narratives used to be part of groups, to be accepted or at least to avoid being rejected and behaving in a way more consistent with their own beliefs. Put in other words, the stories people tell others are not always the same stories they tell themselves. Actually, they often don't believe in the story they tell other people. It is just a *façade* to feel safe and to join in.

The apparent comfort provided by technological innovations has other consequences and not all of them very positive. While we are fighting obesity, we are also giving people all the good reasons not to leave home, including apartment bikes. They can go further with devices such as Meta Quest than with any real means of transportation. And because humans are greedy in nature, no storage capacity is ever sufficient. Thus, this device provides an additional external battery, which you need to hold with you own head. Other than the weight, the danger associated with any batteries is increased by the closeness to your hair and to your head. But consumers would not like to hear this part of the story.

Another aspect to be taken into account is the younger generations' understanding of the limits of the virtual world. Some of them have already serious difficulties in setting their real and virtual lives apart. As a matter of fact, they spend more time in videogames than in real life. After a while, they get both lives mixed up and think that what is possible in the virtual world might also be possible in the real world. One of these people might believe that they can fly just like Spiderman in the game and try to do it for real. In the past, simple advertisements have already led people to take this kind of risk and they were no way as immersive as the technology available today. Such immersion makes all that virtual world feel like reality and thus it makes it harder to set them apart.

Without much technology, a narrative can be source of transportation. When we're transported, our beliefs, attitudes, and intentions are vulnerable to being altered. We can return changed from such journey. It all depends on how we hear the story. It depends on how sensitive we are to the topic, on our relationship with the storyteller, and on the amount of people giving their opinion about the same story and the storyteller. Thus, if the story is of interest to you but you don't trust the source, you are not transported at all. But if you trust the storyteller, you might join in even if the story is not of interest to you. We are still human beings looking for human connections.

We are social, yet lonely people. And we sympathize with people who describe situations we can relate to. This is how we connect with others. We look for similar backgrounds, life experience, and common interests. This is also what explains the lack of content on social media. It is easier to captivate more people when you speak of things everyone can relate to. But this implies a lack of originality. The more original (different) you are, the less people will be able to relate to your story. Knowing that social media viewers spend very little time reading each story and even less time judging the interest of each story to decide which ones they will read, telling the obvious is the right bet to those who post similar stories over and over again.

In a research conducted with one of my graduate students to study social media behavior through the Elaboration Likelihood Model (Petty and Cacioppo 1986), participants were exposed to two types of information. One of them would require reading and information processing while the other one would be a quick read without much content. Only 34 percent of participants decided to go through with reading the long article. The topic being climate change, the big majority of respondents stated that they wouldn't make the effort of reading the article because it would take longer than two minutes. Findings also reinforced the understanding of blind following. Respondents would willingly read what would be recommended by an influencer and, in the absence of one, they would make decisions based on the numbers of views and likes (Karsaklian & Espinosa, 2021). This evidence corroborates the idea that people are unable to make a decision alone. If the topic is of interest to them, they should be able to dive into it without caring about who recommends it and how many people have been reading it. In all the cases, interviewees wouldn't check the original source of the information. Yet, everyone preaches the urgency of taking actions to protect the planet. It is just a narrative; few people are really interested in the topic and even less are taking action.

The climate change narrative has been very trendy ever since Greta Thunberg made a speech at the United Nations. She became synonymous with all noble actions that should be taken to save the planet. People from around the world would admire the courage and lucidity that young person would bring to a whole world of adults and tell experienced scientists and politicians how they should run their countries. Her narratives were depicted as being sharp and spontaneous, which is very rare for a person of her age. Yet, few people wondered how a 13-year-old person could possibly have access to the United Nations, make a long speech, and be rewarded with a stand-up ovation from the world's leaders. Whatever the truth is about her, her narrative and the stories involving her unmistakably address emotions and compassion for the little girl rather than any real concern about the planet.

Emotions rule social media. For three years, I have been observing and testing posts on social media, specifically on LinkedIn, which is the one meant to promote professional contents. Other than observing, I empirically tested different posts with different approaches: professional, personal, self-promotional, challenging content, or inviting to critical thinking. Both methods demonstrated that posts are getting more and more emotional as the ones that feature personal pain or happiness are the ones that collect more likes, comments, and shares.

Most of the posts drawing readers' attention from all cultures are also self-promotional, displaying all the good actions authors perform to other people or to the planet supposedly without seeking any credit, when in reality they are saying "define me," "admire me." In the quest for self-display, self-assertion, and self-approval through other peoples' validation and feeling rewarded by their likes and positive comments, they (humbly) show and document the story they really want to tell "look, I am doing good deeds." Authors of such posts rejoice the comments filled with admiration from their readers whether they know them or not, the goal being to obtain self-approval through external validation; "Look, I am a hero."

Sometimes, authors from these stories didn't even experience the situation they describe; they just saw that somewhere and took authorship just to "look cool."

But as an old Chinese saying states, "good walkers leave no tracks"; that is, if you genuinely do good to others, you don't need to advertise it. You feel internally good, without any need of external validation. This quantitative approach to social validation prompts the following questions: what is more important, numbers or persons? And what is more painful, no gain or losses? When the quest for status in a community takes over personality and content, and where pertinence is judged by the quantity of thumbs up, the community falls into a narrative motivated by ephemeral stories that people will most certainly forget very soon because they will be replaced by fresher ephemeral stories in the following few minutes.

Pictures and videos illustrating long self-satisfactory and emotional stories are thoroughly read and celebrated. But shorter posts questioning status quo, challenging well-set beliefs and inviting to critical thinking are less regarded. Such outcomes should come as a surprise, knowing that unlike platforms such as Facebook, Instagram, or TikTok, LinkedIn is supposed to be a place where people share professional information rather than personal ones. It is worth noting that during the two years of pandemic, there was a shift from professional (rational) to personal (emotional) content on LinkedIn, mainly due to the fact that remote working removed the boundaries between private and professional lives. Thus, when attending a meeting remotely, participants would see part of others' homes, their children, pets, and companions. It was not a big leap to be taken from there to pictures and videos of their pets and children on LinkedIn. This trend perseveres until now. You will find some examples of contents posted on LinkedIn in the appendix of this book.

Whichever the medium, people scan rather than read. That is why words are yielding to images. Emojis are the best example of this substitution. Emojis work well not only because they make interactions easier and faster, but also because they carry emotions. Yet, in a multicultural world, emojis should be inclusive offering a variety of images everyone can relate to. No one can be left out.

Advertisements for medical products do it well. The images portray people enjoying life with friends and family in the parks, practicing sports, enjoying a barbecue or a picnic, as well as being an accomplished professional, while the off voice describes all the side effects of that very medicine which can even be life threatening. Images are what people will imprint and remember more easily because they carry emotions.

Some stories will be forever negative and trigger painful emotions to attract others' attention by making them feel bad. When the same stories about the same victims of history are told time and time again, it nurtures sadness and solidarity with those who have suffered in the past and will, most certainly, keep suffering forever, even if the context has totally changed. It also shows how dependent people are on others, because if no one joins you in your feelings of loss, you can no longer feel as a victim. You end up becoming a victim of yourself, by being defined as someone who will never be anything without the help and the pity of others. You will be known because of your past, not for who you are in reality, not for your accomplishments, nor for what you can bring to others thanks to your skills and personal values. You will always be part of a mass of people with common history, yet with different backgrounds and accomplishments which will rarely be known as individuals.

Victims and heroes are depicted in videogames, which are successful because they offer stories in which we can connect with others while living the ideal life we would choose for ourselves. The goals to pursue are given but the way we reach them depends on our and others' actions. When we team up online, we connect with people pursuing the same goals as us. We connect easily with unknown people because we have goals in common. This is how gamers became a community. In real life, it is harder to find people who have the same goals as us. And sometimes sharing the same goals might lead to competition rather than to collaboration. This is why most people turn to a virtual life. Both videogames and social media trigger addictive consumption because addiction comes from the ability videogames and social media have to fulfill some of human's most basic needs.

As much as the original gift of storytelling was wisdom passed on from the elderly to the younger generations, videogames, social media, and the movies have dramatically changed its role. Stories have always served to pass down lessons on how to live in a society (socialization) from one generation to the next. But today, the stories should be sensational. The films have replaced content with sophisticated special effects. Moviegoers leave the theater with their eyes full of colorful images and with their ears still vibrating to the loud sounds of explosions and unlikely voices. But there is not much to be told about the story narrated by the film.

Storytelling has indeed always been a human practice and helped to bring people together. Technology has changed de nature of the stories and thus of human interactions, but has reinforced the role of storytelling. Rather than waiting for the night when the tribe members would gather around the fire to listen to the stories, we are exposed to them 24/7 through our multiple devices. The big advantage of the contemporary vehicles for storytelling is that they allow sharing our stories with people from all cultures in real time.

Implications for Multicultural Marketing

Communication has always been a need for human survival and its importance is not minor for companies. In an era where consumers speak their minds, companies can go through tough times when there is boycotting.

What's more, what happens in one country is immediately known and followed in other countries. Multinational companies operating in several international markets should deal with their communication in a very careful way to make sure they respect the boundaries without leaving anyone out. The social pressure exerted at the consumer to consumer (C2C) level is as powerful as the one exerted at the consumer to business (C2B) level. Thus, in both international and domestic markets, there is solidarity among consumers when they identify with others and join their cause.

Therefore, both multinational and multicultural marketers should be well aware of the fundamental life goals of their consumers in order to carefully select a corresponding positioning for their brands. Positioning is conveyed by a story about brands' benefits.

Key Takeaways From Chapter 2

- Customer experience has been redefined by online experience, that is, without human interaction.
- The Elaboration Likelihood Model is still pertinent to identify specific interests from specific target markets, mainly those composed of different cultures. It helps to set discourse and real interests apart by isolating the social desirability bias (SDB).
- Social media works well because it is a platform for storytelling where emotions are thoroughly explored.

CHAPTER 3

We Have Always Been in This Together

What's the Story?

Once upon a time, we thought that we were very different at the same time that we thought that we were very much the same. We had a hard time trying to set reality apart from our own beliefs. We didn't know how to tell fate from outcome either; causal effects were not always made clear. It didn't get better when we mixed real and virtual lives either, which also gave us the illusion of a unified one world: we like and buy the same things everywhere. It was time to learn more about ourselves.

We have always been beings of multicultural stories. Drawings from Lascaux cave in France and in the Hands Cave in Argentina are few examples of stories transmitted from generation to generation and tell us part of who we are today and where we come from. As much as we think that we know about our species and multiple races and cultures that have been around for centuries, researchers such as Harari (2015) state that the linear model gives a mistaken impression that, at any particular moment, only one type of human inhabited the earth and that the earlier species were merely older models of ourselves. The author states that the truth is, from about 2 million years ago until around 10,000 years ago, the world was home, at one and the same time, to several human species. As a matter of fact, recent researches published in *Nature* and *Science Advances* demonstrated that ancient humans appear to have reached northwestern China about 2.1 million years ago and lived there for hundreds of thousands of years (Rogers et al. 2020; Warren 2019). A hundred millennia ago, the earth was inhabited by at least six different species of man, that is, different races and different cultures coexisted at the same place.

Today, we know that we belong to the *sapiens* species and we believe that we are superior among all animals. However, a closer look at our children might prove us wrong. Unlike other mammals, human babies depend for many years on their elders for sustenance, protection, and education. This fact has contributed greatly both to humankind's social abilities and also to its unique social problems. It takes a village (tribe) to raise a child (human), as it is said in the popular language, but it also implies consensus on how to raise those who will secure the future of the tribe. Evolution has thus favored those capable of forming strong social ties.

Human children are exposed to a world defined in a binary way: good/bad, right/wrong, safe/dangerous, and clean/dirty. Across cultures and in almost all the religions, people often speak about issues of morality in terms of cleanliness. Expressions such as clean conscience, dirty work, dirty words all demonstrate the metaphorical link between ethical behavior and physical cleansing. This implies the idea of punishment if we are not "clean": the same metaphor applies to honest/dishonest people. If you are honest, you are clean. Based on that, we are now creating a pattern of fear, which rather than bringing people together is setting them apart by pointing out fundamental differences in terms of race and culture. People are suspicious of other people. Although we preach respect for others and inclusiveness, all features that should bring people together thanks to diversity are creating friction and having the opposite effect because they are described as negative/punishment. In doing so, we are creating different tribes defined by race, gender, sex, and culture. In other words, we are pushed to fear and thus reject or even get rid of all those who are not like us; those from other tribes.

Movies, TV shows, and videogames show that very clearly. They are all about fights, wars, and blood. Watching people killing people seems to be entertaining, as announced during *The Terminal List* trailer: "Entertaining from the first to the last shot." We are raising our children in a world of intolerance although the official narrative says the opposite. The best way of pushing people against each other is showing how different (opposed) they are.

Fiction has enabled people not merely to imagine things but to do so collectively. We are able to connect with countless numbers of strangers. That is why we rule the world rather than other animals. Social media, online shopping, online gaming, movies, (social) events, books, and so on: we have so much in common to share, but what we really share are stories about ourselves or stories we want people to believe in, which give us status and power.

For instance, the American science fiction drama television series from Netflix—*Stranger Things*—is getting consumers' attention around the world. In the company's multinational marketing strategy, there was the opening of ephemeral shops to sell the immersive experience and byproducts from the show during the summer tourism peak season in Paris (France), in addition to Chicago and Dallas. In this case, no product adaptation is needed, because fans want the same sensation whichever their culture. There is an identification with the characters and projection into situations depicted in the series. It is all about emotions and belong-ingness to the Stranger Things' community.

It is well known in marketing that emotions are a big driver of consum-ers' attention and intention to buy. For instance, to have more impact on peoples' emotions, several advertisements for products targeting women display a busy single mom being happier thanks to the consumption of the product promoted there. Although the information about the woman's marital status has no connection whatsoever with the product itself and its benefits, the advertisement stresses that feature to gain sympathy to the story they are telling.

Too Big to Be Trusted

Researchers state that there is a critical threshold of 150 people in human organizations below which there is no need for formal ranks and law books to keep order. But once the threshold is crossed, there is need of something else to bring people together and rule their relationships and that is fiction, or common beliefs. In this case, large numbers of strangers can cooperate successfully by believing in common myths. Laws do not rule the world; beliefs do, but they influence each other. The legal system is both a vector and a consequence of cultural beliefs.

Disneyland Paris learned it the hard way. When the Disney's theme park first opened in Europe in 1992, its name was EuroDisney.

The company assumed that half of the visitors would come from European countries other than France. They did, but the French refused to be the other half and boycotted the Disney Park. Among the reasons for such rejection was the standardization of the product: no pets, no picnic, and no alcohol!!! Nothing could be more unFrench!! The marketing communication praising the big size of the Park (much bigger than the existing French parks) and the height of Cinderella's Castle were too offensive to the French who are rarely impressed by superlatives. Disney told the wrong story to the French.

After the big financial losses of the first years of operations, the company decided to rename the park to give it a more "local flavor": Disneyland Paris was the new brand name. It was a good idea to incorporate Paris to the brand name, because Paris was and still is the top tourist destination in the world. But that didn't impress the French either. Even worse, tourists would visit the park during one day and spend the rest of their stay in Paris, which was only 30 km (18 miles) from the French capital city, as stressed in the Park's communication too. Disney told the wrong story to the tourists.

This is not the entire story, but it illustrates very well the case of a multinational corporation that assumed that all Europeans were culturally the same and that everyone in the world would fall for the same standardized and globalized offer. From the French standpoint, the park was too big (and too American) to be trusted. Exactly the same situation happened when Discovery Channel purchased Eurosport, a European TV channel specialized in sports and based in France. The new owner explained that the main advantage of such acquisition was that Eurosport would become part of a bigger organization, with more ambitious goals, which would lead to globalizing their offer. The American team was thrilled at the new challenge, but the European team was all but impressed. That was not the kind of change they were ready to accept. To them, the size of the company would be detrimental to the quality of their services. Had the American acquirers studied the European cultures, they would have been less surprised to see that big quantities, bundles, more for less money, and so on are not what most Europeans value. They would also have understood that all Europeans don't belong to the same culture. Discovery Channel told the wrong story to their internal clients.

When You Feel Threatened, You Make Short-Term Decisions to Survive

Beliefs are shaped by information. You believe in what you know or you think you know. In the old times, people needed to have a very good memory of their territory and know where to find food, how to avoid poisonous food, and where all dangers were. They needed to read other animals' behaviors to anticipate thunderstorms or a dry spell. Everyone should have such mental abilities in order to survive. With evolution, our brains decreased. The more we rely on information brought to us by others, the less we need to think. The less we use our senses, the less sharp they are. We are unable to see very far away without glasses or a handheld telescope, we don't hear very well without our headsets and micros, and we are unable to identify anyone or anything by their smell unless you have a McDonald's, a Subway, or an Abercrombie and Fitch shop nearby. Thanks to classical conditioning, we not only identify these different scents, but we also don't get confused: we know very well when there is a McDonald's or a Subway around without seeing the brand or the logo. We have been exposed to their aroma so many times and for so long that our senses have been trained to recognize them distinctively in any country we go to. We can also distinguish the inviting warm coffee aroma of Starbucks from Dunkin.

In addition to the scents, we are enticed by the stories that link us to these and other brands. We probably remember the first time or the relevant times we went there: if it was in our home country or abroad; if we sampled different products in different countries while buying from the same company.

For instance, if you go to Japan during the cherry blossom season, you will be able to eat a sakura (cherry) donut while drinking a sakura latte at a Starbucks. The company deals with its multinational marketing by adding local products to their standardized ones in each country. Yet, Starbucks could also benefit from the Japanese community in their domestic market by offering the same products during the cherry blossom season. The Japanese consumers living abroad would be grateful to be able to enjoy the flavors they cherish which will most certainly help them to cheer up when they feel homesick. Let's not forget that visiting

Japan to enjoy the cherry blossom season has become a legendary trip: a myth.

A more pleasant widespread contemporary myth is vacations. People are led to believe that fun is an inherent feature of vacations. They wait for them to relax and have fun. That is a myth. You can have great fun at work because you are passionate and love what you do and get deadly bored during vacations. If you do a job that you enjoy, every day is an opportunity for fun and accomplishments. If you don't see every morning as a blossoming opportunity, you'd better change your job. The count-down to vacations can only increase your frustrations with your daily life and make the return to work even harder.

Modern narratives create myths as much as old narratives created myths which persisted for centuries. Today we believe in the 100 percent electric, in the end of prejudice, in life on Mars, and in unity and peace on Earth. But there are as many wars today as there were before. There are religious wars, political wars, and economic wars all around the world. With all these, we wonder if despite all the progress we made, we live better today than during the tribe times.

Implications for Multicultural Marketing

Narratives, stories, emotions, myths, and beliefs easily penetrate our brains and make us believe that all we are exposed to is reality. Our brain is powerful but it is unable to tell reality from thoughts. It reacts the same way. When you are scared at a scene you see in a movie, your brain reacts just like if you were facing the same threat in real life. But because it is a movie, the fear is ephemeral and the relief of not being in that threatening situation in real life sends a different message to your brain and you calm down. The stories of our lives are always this struggle between reality and fiction, danger and safety.

Myths and beliefs are part of the stories of our lives. The more consum-ers from different cultures identify with the myths presented to them, the more loyal to that myth they tend to be. Marketers should show empathy in demonstrating respect and understanding of consumers' main beliefs, while not overusing emotions in their strategies.

Key Takeaways From Chapter 3

- Emotions and senses rule our brains and are useful in marketing.
- Multinational companies use those attributes to entice consumers on global markets.
- The cultural communities addressed abroad can also be profitable in the domestic markets thanks to a well-designed multicultural marketing strategy.

CHAPTER 4

Our Brain; Our Power

What's the Story?

Once upon a time, our three-party-constituted brain had this uncontrollable thirst for stories to help us make sense of our lives. Sense-making would help us in our quest for happiness, ruling our lives, enabling us to face changes, and unlearn deep rooted beliefs such as Pluto doesn't belong to the Solar System.

Stories transport us because our brains do it all the time. Thanks to our storytelling mind, when the body goes to sleep, the mind stays up all night, telling itself stories. While our body is always fixed at a particular point in space-time, our mind is always free to ramble in lands of make-believe. And it does it. We like stories because we can't resist the gravity of alternate worlds (Gottschall 2012). And our dreams are stories we tell ourselves.

Because stories give joy and help in life sense-making, children are natural storytellers. The younger they are, the more limitless is their imagination. Unfortunately, some adults think that they are doing a great job raising their children by correcting them in their stories: dragons don't exist, this is a doll not a plane, stop playing with food, and put away your toys and do your homework. And what if the homework was also a play? How about helping the children to learn through playing? That is perfectly compatible and some schools use these techniques created by knowledgeable and famous experts in children's education.

Children are storytellers by instinct. They are curious and good listeners and observers, qualities that we lose as we grow up and get caught up by the lack of time for doing what is one of the most natural animal instincts: be aware of the surroundings. They create characters and put them in action in a dramatic scenario and don't need to be tutored in the story. Make-believe is as automatic and insuppressible as their dreams.

Children are creatures of story. They see the world through the story's lenses. Any object can turn into a character. Their drawings are stories too and they don't need an adult to correct them because the sky should be blue rather than green. They know very well the real color of the sky, but a blue sky didn't fit in that particular story. The best way of connecting children and parents is still the bedtime stories. This is the opportunity given to adults to dive again in the children's realm.

The same thing happens when parents are surprised to see their child playing with the box longer than with the toy that came inside. For the child, the box is a house, a car, a castle, a little place just for themselves. The toy is part of another story. Because adults use less and less imagination (everything is already formatted, given and ready to use), they have a hard time understanding how important mind- and personality-shaping drawing is to a child. The stories they tell in their drawings can go a long way and tell much about their vision of their lives and their surroundings. Drawings tell more than what words can express (Karsaklian 1995). When adults criticize or tell the children to change or "correct" their drawings, they are changing the story the children meant to tell. This is the first encounter between the children and their parents' ignorance.

The Danish company Lego has long understood the role of children and parents in playing with toys. Rather than producing and selling toys, they sell bricks to build the world. Their products are pretty much standardized and sold around the world. And with concepts addressing consumers ranging from 6 months to more than 77 years old they bring families together for several hours of fun, creativity, and learning. Their concept based on building is so successful that companies use their bricks to stimulate and measure creativity and to reinforce teamwork, while engineering schools use them to build prototypes. By doing so, Lego company tries to satisfy all types of consumers independently of their respective cultures thanks to licenses from stories everyone is attached to: Harry Potter, Star Wars, NBA, Batman, just to name a few.

Adults are not always of big help in understanding their children's stories, but they still know that the best thing in life is play. Adults play (tennis, yoga, fitness, golf, casinos, bars, dance clubs, videogames, lottery, poker, and even the games on their phones such as Candy Crush) but call them differently: looking after their health, networking, killing time, trying to become a millionaire, and so on. Several international business contracts are signed in golf clubs. It is easier to size up people and create connections outside of the office. And after we played golf together, we have stories to share. The games might change, be updated and adapted to different ages and cultures, but the bedrock remains the story.

Stories are like flight simulators: we get trained safely to what will happen in real life with the big challenges of the social world. When we experience fiction, our neurons are firing as much as they would if we were actually faced with those emotions in real life. Our immersion in fictional problem solving can improve our ability to deal with real problems. Our brains can't tell the difference between fiction, thoughts, and reality. Fiction is a powerful and ancient virtual reality technology that simulates the big dilemmas of human life. Whenever we get into a story, we are teleported into another universe. We are attracted to stories that make us deal with problems. A story that goes smoothly sounds uninteresting. Fiction is an escape but it takes us to an imaginary world of struggles and concerns. We suffer with the characters; we cry and laugh with them too.

As much as people would like to relate to the stories depicted in movies, they also enjoy experiencing fear without feeling threatened. This explains why dramas are successful and why the most well-known classics are tragedies. The Greek tragedies were already highly appreciated. Additionally, the most awarded movies in film festivals are dramas, mainly those inspired by true stories. Moviegoers suffer with the characters because their brains are exposed to scenes of high emotional charge. At the same time, they feel relieved that the same drama is not actually happening to them.

Happiness Depends on Your Reaction to External Events. If You Take Everything Personally, You'll Always Be Unhappy

Had Walt Disney defined his company's mission as a producer of cartoons for children, it wouldn't have lasted long. Instead, he defined his company's mission as bringing happiness to millions of people. He was wise enough to have created characters with animals embodying human characteristics. Mickey and Minnie Mouse, Donald Duck, Goofy, and so on could never been accused of stereotyping.

With the growth of the company came the diversification of their products and Disney got into the animated industry, depicting stories written by international authors, most of these stories constituting works of international classical literature. Few examples are Snow White, which was a 19th-century German folk tale, written by the Brothers Grimm; The Aristocats was inspired by the true story of a Parisian family of cats having inherited a fabulous fortune; and Peter Pan was a fictional character created by the Scottish novelist and playwright Sir J. M. Barrie. These animations would enable children and their families to have an overview of the stories written by authors from around the world about stories from around the world.

But Walt Disney's heirs and successors, being recently scared to death at any kind of backlash or boycott from their audiences, decided to block the access to *Peter Pan* and *The Aristocats* among other stories to the under seven years old because they would convey "negative depictions and/or mistreatment of people or cultures." In their hasty decisions to please everyone and avoid any causes of insurgence, they allowed themselves to violate one of the most fundamental values of storytelling: authenticity. *The Little Mermaid*, story written by the Danish author Hans Christiansen in 1837, depicts a red-haired, blue-eyed, pale-skinned creature which is half woman, half fish. Because the Vikings were the ancestors of the Danes, this little character looked just like the Vikings and would live in the seas because the Vikings were great navigators. That is why one of the most visited monuments in the world is the Little Mermaid statue facing the sea in Copenhagen.

But the Disney team decided to update the story to the current trends and flavors in the United States and launched a movie, rather than an animation, with an African American Ariel, starred by actress Halle Bailey, who is physically very different from a descendent of Vikings. And this is where the backlash came from.

The decision made by Disney's management also demonstrated a total lack of creativity. Africa is the most multicultural continent in the world and all African countries have fascinating stories to be told, which would deserve exceptional film productions like those made by Disney. If the company's goal was to pay tribute to the African American community, rather than recycling or updating a Danish classical literature in all wrong ways possible, it would have been wiser to have studied the richness of the different African cultures and created an original version of a movie based on African tales which would not only be successful and profitable but would also, and more importantly, be authentic. This way, African Americans would have felt respected, appreciated, and reconnected with their deepest cultural roots.

Hopefully, Disney learned their lesson and will be less greedy and more focused on happiness from now on.

Humans are a greedy species. What they have is never enough. They want more power, more money, more possessions, and more territory. The more they have, the more they want to have. People want to be celebrities, seen in the media and followed by the mob on social media. The value of people comes from numbers: their fortune, their followers, their connections, the likes, the shares, and so on. No one cares about who the followers are and what the contents are: people mechanically like and share and this is how the numbers grow exponentially in a few hours. People don't really read or fact-check. On social media, the shorter, the better. That is not a place to require much information processing.

Because people always want more, they are never happy. The more they have, the more they risk and the more they are haunted by worries. They can't be happy. If fame and fortune were the way to happiness, celebrities wouldn't kill themselves. Humankind is doomed to suffer and the "tyranny of the expected" can hold us hostage in the present moment (Gottshall 2012). Plato said that motivations come from needs and needs come from scarcity. When we don't have what we need, we are happy to fight for it. But once we've got it, we have no more motivation, because there is no need, and life seems pointless.

The fear of losing what we have is well assessed by insurance companies and law firms. You install a security system in your home and subscribe to home, life, and car insurance. You get the lawyers' phone number in case you are involved in a car accident or if your home is violated. You protect your possessions more than you protect yourself. At the same time, you are already considering buying a new car, changing your TV set to a bigger one, and moving to a better house. It is a never-ending cycle of satisfaction and fear yielding to each other at each purchase.

Ambition is inherent in humans. We always want more and this is what gives sense to our lives. The pursuit of success and thus, happiness, relates to the highest levels of human needs, which are self-actualization needs. We tend to perfection and this is why we are always in the quest for more and better. This is also how more became better; ours is a world defined by quantity rather than quality.

Although Maslow's pyramid of needs (1943) has been criticized, we can define several customers' behaviors in the light of his five levels of needs. It seems that the most salient needs to be satisfied today are belonging and safety. These are not at the highest levels of the pyramid of needs. Security is at the second level, yet all the fear instilled on us today addresses the need of security and this is why we spend considerable amount of money in security products. Belonging is even clearly demonstrated by the power of social media. People belong to communities in social media as they used to belong to tribes in the old times.

And with the segmentation of the society based on demographic criteria, people today belong to tribes that set them apart: women, men, transgender, LGBTQ+, black, white, and so on. We also witness the emergence of the gamers' tribe where socialization is made possible thanks to online games where the gamers can meet and play with other gamers from around the world.

This notion of greed is also in line with Buddhist philosophy. It outlines the roots of human suffering to be the one that gets caught up in the endless cycle of desire and attachment. We desire happiness and attach our entire life's worth to feeling fulfilled in our careers, relationships, and celebrations. More importantly, we decide how to best present that glossy illusion of perfection to our followers and friends online to validate our existence and purpose on Earth.

What happens to our psyche when we fall short? Everybody wants to be happy, of course; it is in our nature but when we put so much pressure on ourselves and the means to achieve that goal, the ends are often met with disappointment. If we are expected to be happy every single moment of every single day, those unrealistic expectations can end up being the source of big disappointment.

You Rule Your Brain. Not the Other Way Around

All human beings are born with brains divided into three parts: the cortex (logic), the amygdalian (emotion), and the reptilian brain (instinct). The cortex (the cerebral hemispheres) handles learning, abstract thought, and imagination. It helps us to make intellectual assessments after the age of seven. The amygdalian brain is responsible for our emotions. This is also the part of the brain that makes us enjoy stories, because stories without emotions are unable to lure humans. We are happy, sad, feel sorry, laugh, and cry, thanks to the amygdalian brain.

Because the limbic system (the hippocampus, amygdale, and the hypothalamus) deals with emotions, it often takes over the cortex because humans are much more likely to allow their hearts to guide their behavior than reason. Manipulation rests on the limbic part of the brain, leading people by their emotions. It is impossible to manipulate others based on reason. The cortex is responsible for our thinking ability. This is when we analyze, criticize, and are rational about what we are faced with, leaving little room to blind following.

The third part is the reptilian brain (the brainstem and the cerebellum). Because it is responsible for our survival and reproduction, our most fundamental instincts, it takes over the other two parts of our brain. In a battle between logic, emotion, and instinct, the reptilian brain always wins. The reptilian part of our brain is responsible of our animal nature. This is where our animal instincts are generated. When we react without thinking just per reflex, it is the reptilian brain that is at command.

These three parts of our brains create mental highways that take us to our understanding of our lives and the world we live in. Such highways create our mental routines and the reactions we have to our daily challenges. The routine actions are mechanical; no need of too much thinking or emotion, but it is when we are confronted with unexpected situations that our reptilian brain reacts automatically and in the short term. Instincts along with long-lasting and deep-rooted beliefs based on myths shape our immediate reactions to specific situations, without allowing time for a rational analysis.

Levis-Strauss (1979) stated that all mythology is dialectic in its attempt to make cognitive sense out of the chaotic data provided by nature and that this attempt traps human imagination in a web of dualisms. Myth is a form of language and underneath language lies the binary nature of the brain itself: right and left. Life and death are two inevitable dichotomies produced by the brain that has two lobes and controls two eyes, two hands, and two legs. "We are split creatures literally by nature, and we organize data like a simple digital machine" (p. 21). Our common sense is binary; the simplest and most efficient way to process experience seems to be by dividing in half.

The Solar System Myth Falls Apart

Of all well-known mythologies, the Greek myths and the Roman mythology are the ones that stand out. Being polytheistic cultures, they could refer to several Gods, each one representing different facets of human nature. Not only do we learn about them in school but they are also part of our current lives. Most of the stories we know are rooted in these two cultures. Mythology is a collection of myths, especially one belonging to a particular culture. As a matter of fact, ancient Greek mythology is a vast and fascinating group of legends about Gods and Goddesses, heroes and monsters, warriors and fools, which were an important part of everyday life in the ancient world. Greek myths explained everything from religious rituals to the weather and gave meaning to the world that people saw around them. While many of these myths are made-up tales, for example, about King Midas who would turn everything he would touch into gold, other stories like the Trojan War epic have a basis in historical facts. The Romans, belonging to a different culture, have indeed inherited from the Greek mythology but extended and adapted it to their own stories. These myths, although often appearing as simple stories filled with valiant heroes, maidens in distress, and a host of all-powerful Gods, are much more than fictional stories. The Gods of the Greeks and Romans were anthropomorphic, exhibiting many human qualities such as love, hate, and jealousy, and because of this, their people could relate to them and understand their relationship to the rest of the world as well as their connection to the Gods. The lesson to be learned was often that one must meet one's destiny with strength, determination, and nobility.

It is noteworthy that myths are different from fairytales and folktales. For all people, in many ways, myths made life bearable by providing security because they dealt with important issues: the creation of the world, the nature of good and evil, and even the afterlife. And, for this reason, these tales have stood the test of time and become part of our present day across all cultures. The best example of it is the names of the planets constituting the Solar System, named after Roman Gods and Goddesses: Mercury, Venus, Mars, Jupiter, Saturn, Neptune, Uranus. Pluto was there too, until it was recently discovered that the last planet of the Solar System was not part of it. This is a wonderful example of the evolution of science and knowledge. But it can be shocking to all those who were obliged to learn the name of all the eight planets by heart and in the right order of proximity with Earth at school. The Solar System myth falls apart.

While much of the Roman mythology was derived from their neighbors and predecessors, the Greeks, still defined the rich history of their culture adding their own vision of Gods and history. For example, the myth about Romulus and Remus having been fed and raised by a she-wolf tells the story of the foundation of Rome and of the Roman Empire.

The use of the Greek and Roman mythologies in marketing is with no doubt of precious value. Other than the multiple bestseller books describing sexual differences explained by the fact that women come from the planet Venus and men come from Mars, there are also products such as feminine razors brand benefitting from the Roman *Goddess,* Venus, whose functions encompassed love, beauty, desire, sex, and fertility.

Nike takes its inspiration from the Greek Goddess of Victory "Nicé." As she was winged, Nike's logo is derived from the goddess' wings' "swoosh," which symbolizes the sound of speed, movement, power, and motivation, while Midas fixes your car.

The French company Danone (Dannon in the United States) launched a Greek yogurt named Oikos. In the advertisement, we see Ares, the Greek God of war, arriving at Oikos' building as if he was arriving at home because Oikos in Greek means house, family, household, and home, where he would fight all the enemies of "possibly the best yogurt in the world."

The reference to myths with a touch of humor entices the customers because it generates happy emotions and helps to learn about the products as well as to easily remember the brand name.

Change Is How We Grow

Based on that, Rapaille (2007) states that little learning or memory takes place without emotion. No change can happen without emotion and that is why advertising and politics use emotions to influence people's decisions. During election campaigns, and in an attempt to reach out to voters' emotions, we see some politicians' children pleading to vote for their parents in their advertisements on TV while it is obvious that the children don't know what they are talking about.

Yet, more often than not, fear is the emotion used by those who aim at an immediate change. Little rational or technical information is given, but the images are powerful to make people sensitive to what they are exposed to. Also, by repetition, the audience is more likely to memorize the images. Fear is one of the primitive emotions because it is linked to survival. With a simple operating conditioning process, people are rewarded when they do what they are told to do or are punished when they don't comply.

When people want to change and create new mental highways through paradigm shifts, expecting new attitudes and behaviors to follow, they sometimes don't understand that they can't accomplish such a change without emotion (Rapaille, 2007). Strong emotions are linked to survival and primitive fear. Depending on the culture, change can be a reward or a punishment. In risk-averse cultures, change is perceived as being threatening and tends to be avoided; the person trying to introduce changes is not well seen and faces strong resistance to change. Such a resistance can be either passive or active. On the other hand, in risk-taking cultures, change is well received and those who innovate are praised. Unlike common belief, resistance to change doesn't always come from the lower levels of hierarchy. Indeed, we are always told about the challenges faced by managers to implement change in their companies. But managers can also be resistant to change because they might feel like their position will be at stake (lack of power and of control) and even if their teams would request changes, the manager will refrain from putting them into place.

The willingness to resist or to change has little to do with human intelligence. Human brain capabilities are often associated to people's intelligence. Intelligence rests in awareness and the ability and the willingness to learn. Emotional intelligence (Salavoy and Mayer 1990) implies self-awareness and the ability of adjusting to multiple environments, while cultural intelligence (Ang et al. 2006) enables people to understand and adjust to diverse cultural settings. People with high cultural intelligence are open to cultural diversity and enjoy listening, observing, and learning from others. Emotional and cultural intelligences are more extensively explained in Chapter 5.

Culturally intelligent people are culturally curious people. They enjoy traveling to countries they are unfamiliar with. They like to discover new practices and people from other cultures. They don't mind being in a place where they can't speak the language and are unfamiliar with the food. In addition, they enjoy joining in new rituals. The contact with people from other cultures makes them feel like being part of something different and they understand that rituals are the glue that keeps people together. On the other hand, people who are not culturally curious see no use in getting to know people from other cultures, keep practicing rituals from their own culture, and don't enjoy travelling, learning about new languages, or different kinds of foods.

None of them are to be criticized. Rather, we should understand that they belong to different tribes and the stories they tell are very different. If we imagine both types partaking in a same trip, culturally curious people will very much enjoy getting to know new foods, new places, and new people, while not culturally curious people will remain among themselves, avoiding eating unknown foods and speaking to local people, and will probably remain hungry and bored throughout the trip. For the first ones, the end of the trip will be a bit sad and they will try to keep in touch with those they met abroad. For the second ones, it will be a relief and they will cherish their home more than ever.

Implications for Multicultural Marketing

The scientific approach to understanding tribes and cultures is imperative if we want to understand human behavior. Independent of our lifestyles, we are all consumers and inhabitants of the same planet. With the globalization of stories, we are exposed to similar situations and should be well aware of how to face them as well as of the consequences of our decisions. The missions, positioning, and concepts created by companies can make sense in multinational markets as well as in multicultural markets if they address universal rather than culture-specific values. Happiness is one universal value, which, while not always defined the same way, can be generated by consumption too.

Key Takeaways From Chapter 4

- For mythology to be used in marketing, it should make sense to consumers.
- Sense-making comes from familiarity with the cultural reference system.
- The pivotal role of emotions in learning should not be neglected: you can't teach those who don't engage in learning. Marketers want consumers to learn about their products and brands.

CHAPTER 5

When Emotions Take Over Science

What's the Story?

Once upon a time, we believed in Gods and myths. We also thought that multiculturalism and multiracialism were the same concept, but science changed our reference systems and took us to a more rational understanding of the same stories about life, culture, and race. Yet, emotions kept ruling humans' perception of reality, which is merged with the need of material possessions.

With the advent of science in the 17th century, we have rejected mythology as a product of superstition and primitive minds. Yet now we are coming to a fuller appreciation of the nature and role of myth in human history. At that time, it was necessary for science to build itself against the old generations of mythical and mystical thought, and it was thought that science could only exist by turning its back upon the world of senses. We entered a "real world" of mathematical properties, which could only be grasped by the intellect and which were entirely at odds with the false testimony of the senses. But now, more and more sense data are being integrated into scientific explanation as something which has a meaning and which can be explained.

The French philosopher René Decartes (1637) had already stated that mind and soul were two separate things and that emotions and rationality were not to be mixed when explaining human behavior. Of course, his theory was then questioned and proven wrong by modern philosophers. Without any doubt, in marketing we know that no purchase decision is totally rational. Whatever the product category in view, there is always a part of rationality as well as a part of emotion in consumers' decisions. Depending on the situation and on what is at stake, one of the parts takes precedence over the other.

Atmospherics marketing is a fair illustration of the role of emotions and sensations in buying decisions. As a matter of fact, the term coined by Philip Kotler in 1973 is defined as the use of the five senses to entice consumers in the point of sale and it has been widely used by companies as part of their identity. Chemists are now able to tell us that each smell or each taste has a certain chemical composition and give us the reasons why subjectively some smells or some tastes feel to us as having something in common and why some others seem widely different. Marketers know that smells and tastes are part of their brand identity: that unique warm aroma of coffee, like no other, invites us to walk into a Starbucks every morning. We always know when there is a Subway or a McDonald's around because they don't spread the same scent and you just can't walk past an Abercrombie and Fitch shop without noticing their perfume. The aroma of fresh baked cookies in their shops is what made Crumbl's brand awareness grow very fast on social media.

Multisensory marketing is of utmost importance in attracting consumers' attention. A recent study conducted by Sixième Son demonstrated that sonic brand cues have more impact on brand attention (25 percent) than characters (18 percent), celebrities (8 percent), font (4 percent), and color (3 percent). Sound becomes even more pertinent when the sound-oriented media flourish. Indeed, the use of podcasts, TikTok, voice apps, and so on intensifies the attention and thus the identification of sounds as a signature of brands. This evidence also brings back an old media story. When radio was the only medium of information and entertainment. Radio speakers were selected depending on their voices, radio novels actors needed to stress dramatic voices to convey their (invisible) body language as well, and advertising should demonstrate all the pleasure of consumption by the sound alone. We could hear a bottle of Coke being opened and the thirst went away!

For many years, marketers tried to make their products as silent as possible, believing that noises annoyed their consumers. Most of Dyson's vacuum cleaners' communication is based on silence. Yet, it was found that when the door of a car doesn't make noise, consumers have the feeling that it had remained unlocked. The sound offers closure. Yet, multicultural marketers should ensure the understanding of different cultural references. Thus, the same sound might not trigger the same kind of memories, and of meaning, to different cultures. Because of history, geography, and a whole reference system, similar sounds can evoke different emotions. Put in other words, the same sound might tell a different story to consumers from different cultures, because the same sound can refer to positive situations in some cultures but it can also refer to negative references in some others. Sounds tell stories as they remind people of their experiences. Sounds, as much as images and scents, trigger emotions and bring back stories from the past.

Emotions are also indispensable in the learning process. Emotions imply engagement and the latter is what leads to learning. It is indeed possible to distinguish teaching from learning. The teacher can lecture, but if the students are not engaged they will learn nothing. Rapaille (2007) states that emotion is the crucial energy required for the imprinting of cultural archetypes and, in general, for learning. In other words, without emotions there are no imprints, that is, there is no memorization and no impact of what was experienced in our lives.

Cultural archetypes are the laws of the culture in which we are born that pertain to human relationships and human organizations. The unconscious behavior patterns caused by imprints can be split among two categories: universal archetypes and cultural archetypes. The patterns that enable people to meet their biological survival needs are universal archetypes. Imprints that enable people to better understand human conditions are cultural archetypes.

The strongest the emotion associated with an imprint, the stronger the archetype. Because the ability to learn is key to intelligence, emotion is key to intelligence. There are different types of intelligence, including emotional intelligence (EI) and cultural intelligence. The term emotional intelligence was coined by Salavoy and Mayer in 1990 and states that emotions can drive our behavior and impact people (positively and negatively). Put in other words, EI is learning how to manage emotions, both our own and others'. Later, Goleman (1995) extensively popularized the concept. Added to intelligence quotient (IQ), EI is very appropriate, because EI helps to read, decode, and understand peoples' behaviors through the understanding of their emotions. At the same time, your emotional stability enables you to empathize with other people, which is crucial in human relationships. For instance, in Denmark, a country very open to other cultures, empathy courses have been required in schools since 1993. That is also the great advantage of multiculturalism. What seems to be a new trend or an innovation in one culture can be an old practice in some other cultures. Thereby, the more we interact with other cultures, the more we can learn from them.

This ability to empathize with others is of fundamental importance in multicultural settings. Interacting with people from other cultures requires the ability of understanding the underlying reasons for different behaviors and the acceptance of differences. More accurately, it is cultural intelligence that enables people to learn and to feel comfortable in a multicultural world. Cultural intelligence (CQ) was defined by Earley and Ang (2003) as the ability to adapt to new cultural settings. Their concept was materialized by a model created by Livermore (2010) and is composed of four practical aspects: the CQ drive represents the fundamental reasons why someone would willingly be exposed to a different culture. The knowledge CQ describes the time and the effort the individual puts in learning and understanding the foreign culture. The strategy CQ defines a strategy to better interact with people from that specific foreign culture. Finally, the Action CQ defines an action plan to operationalize the strategy and is mainly based on communication skills of the foreigner when interacting with the locals.

From Having to Being

Although tangible possessions are still of utmost importance in most cultures, consumers are also trying to define themselves as beings of opinion. We live in a world of opinions rather than facts, of emotions rather than rationality, of assumptions rather than knowledge. This takes us back to the world of myths and beliefs opposed to the scientific critical thinking.

Science is rationality, the analysis of facts and the understanding of specific phenomena. Emotion is all the opposite. When dominated by emotions, people lose their objectivity and rationality and thus react by impulsion. We live in a narcissistic society where everyone likes to listen to their own voices and neglects or rejects opinions different from theirs. It is a society defined by fame and celebrity at the very individual level. People are defined by the numbers of followers, likes, and shares.

This creates a stream of thoughts accepted by a "majority" of followers and anyone who disagrees with such beliefs is ruled out or canceled.

This is how we saw the emergence of cancel culture, which is an unofficial individual censorship opposed to the freedom of speech. This can also be translated into "if you are not on my side you are against me." There are no other options.

Admittedly, we are led to believe that we are drowning in a mass of constant information, which is difficult to filter in order to make appropriate choices. We might be exposed to information 24/7 but when moving from channel to channel and across media, whether social or not, we hear the same story: the mainstream narrative about the same topics, always and everywhere. And because the attention span is currently estimated as six seconds, if you don't grab people's interest in those few seconds, you lose them. Thus, the more dramatic the tone of your story, the higher the likelihood of attracting your audience's attention is.

Rationality yields to individual susceptibility, fact-checking, and questioning of widespread beliefs. But when emotions take over reason, it is much easier to generate followers behind a well-told dramatic story. Rationality doesn't yield to manipulations, but emotions do. All stories appeal to emotions and this is why people pay attention to them and believe in them.

In democratic societies, rationality should prevail if we want to enjoy constructive debates. Whenever emotions are introduced, there is no possible debate because people take everything personally and rather than arguing and counter arguing factually, they defend themselves by attacking others. Argumentations turn into accusations. This is all the opposite of argumentative rhetoric. We live in a world of personal opinion instead of a world of facts which would be ruled by science. What is called information today is more of an opinion given by people paid to give their own opinion, often without any expertise on the topic. Political ideology is the utmost expression of lack of rationality and emotional discrimination because we are required to pick only one side and treat all the other sides as enemies no matter what they say and do. We vote for those who tell us the stories we want to hear.

In this context, information is a driver of behavior but we rarely check its source and tend to take it as absolute truth. In times of crisis and stress, people tend to believe even more unconditionally in what they hear. For instance, during the pandemic, people stopped buying food from restaurants they used to eat in every day before, because they thought that they could be infected. And yet, these places were even cleaner and safer with the new restrictions and regulations than before the pandemic as they should comply with new sanitary rules. But that would be a rational understanding of reality. Because most communication is now vehiculated by (social) media, immediacy takes over critical thinking. It takes time to think.

Multiculturalism and Multiracialism Took Us Where We Are Today

All civilizations have been slaves and slavers some time in their history. Whenever another culture would take over, the local population would be reduced to servants. Egypt is a good example, having been conquered numerous times over the centuries by Assyrians, Persians, Macedonians, Romans, Arabs, Mamluks, Turks, and the British, who established their own laws in a country that had been historically ruled by the Pharaoh laws. In the contemporary world, war prisoners are treated like slaves. They are used to do the most mineable jobs without knowing for how long they will live. They can be killed at any moment, because they belong to the enemy's side.

When it comes to race and culture, there is a fundamental difference between slavery and war prisoners. For example, during the black slavery era, several Africans tragically died from illnesses, cruelty, abuse, and mistreatment, but there has never been an intention of elimination of the race—the slavers needed their slaves—as opposed to war prisoners who are killed with the goal of exterminating the enemies' race and culture.

All African empires have been slavers. In Western Africa, in 1900, there were still seven million slaves sold among African countries. In the Zanzibar markets alone, there was traffic of 1.5 million slaves. That is why when Europeans and North Americans chose to import slaves, they turned to Africa because there was already a well-developed slave trade system exporting them mainly to the Middle East. As a matter of fact, in the Arab-Muslim Empire, there were between 15 and 20 million slaves from 1650 to 1920. Most of them were women, sold by their own fathers, not for work, but for sexual satisfaction. The more women they had, the more powerful they would prove to be. But also, the more women they would have, the more eunuchs they would need, which was also a sign of higher social rung (Harari 2015).

This takes the conversations about slavery far beyond the dichotomy of white slavers and black slaves. Sadly, slavery is not over. It is known that there are more slaves in the world today than during the 17th century. And they are from all cultures, races, genders, and ages. Yet, slavery is a forbidden practice today, as opposed to the 17th century, when it was legal.

In fact, what is called "modern slavery" is a wide-spread, global problem (Kara 2009, 2012). The International Labor Organization (ILO) along with the Walk Free Foundation (2018) estimates that about 40.3 million people are in modern slavery (ILO 2017). Indeed, there are more slaves in the contemporary world than was ever the case in the last 500 years (Bales et al., 2009). Modern slavery is not limited to the Global South. It is estimated that about 400,000 people are currently enslaved in the US, and that at least 1 million people are modern slaves across Europe (www.globalslaveryindex.org). Modern slavery is often invisible to those who live, work and consume in the same communities. Many of these people are victims of human trafficking and are enslaved in industries, such as, domestic work, agriculture, restaurants/food service, and the sex trade, with women and girls representing the largest share of forced labor victims.

Biological and cultural differences are a scientific reality; however, no race or ethnicity is superior or inferior. This is a human invention based on their own myth of social differences. For example, Hindus who adhere to the caste system believe that cosmic forces have made one caste superior to another because they were created from different parts of Purusa's body. This is probably the heritage from the Indo-Aryan invasion of the Indian subcontinent about 3,000 years ago subjugating the local population. The invaders established a stratified society in which they occupied the leading positions, although they were few in number. And on behalf of purity, mixing of castes was forbidden, which was the best way of keeping everyone locked in their own castes forever, generation after generation. Another example of the inception of purity is the ancient Chinese myth which tells that when the Goddess Nü Wa created humans from earth, she kneaded aristocrats from fine yellow soil whereas commoners were formed from brown mud. Thus, the color of the skin became a factor of social distinction. This relates to the concept of "cultural contamination" (Harari 2015).

Although cultural contamination might sound as a very negative expression, it is the way cultures evolve. Cultural and social differences within the predominant culture are what make cities and countries multicultural. Unlike widespread beliefs, cultures are not static. They evolve throughout time and an accelerator of this process is the interaction with other cultures. Whenever we are exposed to other cultures, we learn from the local people as much as we convey our ideas and practices to them. Some of these learnings are remembered and adopted, while some others are forgotten. Those that are adopted are incorporated in the foreign culture and after a while, they become part of the local culture. This is easily visible in language, when words and expressions are imported from other cultures, as well as in the eating habits. Thus, pizza is predominant in the United States thanks to the Italian influence and Americans are eating spicier foods as Latin American cultures penetrate the market more intensively. The same can be said about the United Kingdom where tikka masala became the most popular food. In France, words such as *arrêt* have been replaced by *stop* in the traffic signs and *stationnement* by *parking*.

As horrible as any kind of cultural submission can be, this is also a factor of cultural evolution. It is because people from different cultures inhabited the same places at the same time that there are mixed races and culturally mixed people leading to multiculturalsm in all countries. We might think that this is a recent trend, yet it is rooted in the past with colonization and immigration. The role of science is to describe, not to judge. But putting people in a constant emotional state makes them fiercely judgmental and constantly in confrontation rather than enjoying all the benefits multiculturalism can bring to them. It is easier to narrow down all existence to only two opposing forces (men X women, black X white, heterosexual X homosexual…) and thus push the understanding of the world limited to either one or the other options. Trying to explain the past with a present mindset is just not realistic and it can only lead to misunderstanding and more ignorance. It is a violation of the historical context and the reinforcement of myths that can't be explained by science because they are just myths.

Those Who Know, Lead; Those Who Don't Know, Follow

Because we are locked in our communities, we ignore what happens outside of them. Had the Aztecs, Mayas, Incas, and Toltecs some knowledge of the existence of South America and better awareness of their surroundings, chances are that they would have known what the Spaniards had already done to their neighbors and might have resisted the Spanish conquest more successfully. As the Spaniards had an overview of what the continent looked like and of the peoples inhabiting it, they were more powerful than the local empires. Ironically, the Spanish missions were outsiders, outnumbered by the local warriors, and yet they won and imposed their empire. The lack of awareness and knowledge of their surroundings cost the local peoples their empires. Thanks to a close cooperation with science, these new empires wielded much power and changed the world to a large extent. This gave them the feeling that they were of a superior race, and they believed it (Harari 2015).

A peripheral vision is critical to power, to clairvoyance, and to strategy. Whenever we are overfocused on our own communities, we don't see what others can offer, we miss opportunities of collaboration, and we tend to confront, just like in the old days: "if you are not like me, you are against me." What's more, it reinforces favoritisms and discrimination because everyone will aim at protecting their own community against others. Yet, this doesn't prevent conflicts and discrimination within the same community.

Indeed, blind rejection, just by principle, can lead to big losses. When Christopher Columbus approached the king of Portugal with the proposal that he finance the fleet that would sail westward to find new trade routes to East Asia, he was turned down. Such explorations were as risky as costly with no guarantee of success and any return on investment. Columbus kept pitching his idea to potential investors in Italy, France, and England, and they all declined for the same reasons.

He then tried the Spanish royalty and Queen Isabella decided to invest in his endeavor, and as we already know, this is how Spaniards conquered America (Harari 2015).

Rather than being admired and respected, Columbus is currently blamed for having discovered and colonized America. His statues are destroyed in some of the countries he settled in and the traditional Columbus Day's celebrations have been forbidden as well. While Columbus is criticized for being a white male and a slaver, which became almost synonyms, what is less known and ironically not celebrated today is that the decision maker was a woman!

It is not questionable that colonization had terrible aspects and that it was, in all countries, very disrespectful of the native populations. Most of them were almost exterminated. North America, Latin America, Australia, New Zealand, Canada, and all African countries are few examples of the heartless practices of colonizers. Today, peoples from these countries try to remove the past history, reject the colonizers, and even want to take revenge. Yet, and as we all know, nothing has only one side. Let's imagine that the British and the Dutch wouldn't have colonized North America, Australia, and New Zealand. Let's also imagine that the Spaniards hadn't colonized most of Latin America, same for the Portuguese for Brazil and Africa along with France and England. What would these countries be like today?

They were most likely to be colonized by other cultures, speak other languages, practice different rituals, and so forth. But someone would have taken over the native populations anyway. It is an illusion to think that those countries would have remained pristine until today. So, when we protest against the colonizers, what is it that we want?

Do we want to rewrite history and tell a different story about the colonization era? It won't change the reality. Because humans have a contradictory mind: peoples around the world move against their own history at the same time as they enjoy the country they were born, raised, and live in today. They want to change only some parts of their country's history's narrative, the ones that align with the contemporary narratives, while keeping all the rest as is.

We should also consider the fact that we are getting so globalized and so unified that perhaps it wouldn't matter who colonized whom, because right now we are subjected to a different kind of imperialism that is trying to make all cultures look alike. Thus, trying to rewrite history is not only a waste of time, but also and mainly an illusion.

Problems Can Either Upset You or Inspire You

Technology doesn't seem to be helping to understand multiculturalism. With around 20 million international flights operated every day, we still question cultural differences and don't know how to deal with them. When it comes to multinational marketing, some companies learned it the hard way. McDonald's believed in a globalized world of consumers and tried to push the same menu they had in the United States to several countries, mainly in Europe, where the company assumed that those western cultures were not so different. They were severely boycotted in France and Italy, countries that praise food above everything else and where eating and feeding are not synonymous. The company learned to mix adaptation with standardization, which enabled it to continue their operations in these countries.

On the other hand, the company was more careful when dealing with eastern cultures, conducted market research, and adapted their products to local habits. In India, for example, food consumption was influenced by people's religious beliefs. Accordingly, McDonald's has dropped beef and pork from its menus, conforming to the religious beliefs of Hindus and Muslims, who make up most of India's population. Instead, it has numerous vegetarian versions of some of its American classics, like the McVeggie burger and McSpicy Paneer, as well as chicken offerings. On the value menu, the McAloo Tikki burger, made from a potato-based patty, is a top seller, accounting for as much as 25 percent of the restaurants' total sales in India (Malhotra et al. 2017). In this example, McDonald's practiced both multinational and multicultural marketing—multinational by adapting to the Indian market and multicultural by adapting to different needs within the Indian population.

History teaches us that what seems to be just around the corner may never materialize due to unforeseen barriers. As much as we have fantasized about living on Mars and space colonies right after the first mission to space was successful, nothing like that has happened yet.

However, no one had seen the power and penetration of the Internet and the pervasion of technology in creating smartphones, social media, and remote working, studying, and socializing in times of Covid pandemic. Nor has the pandemic been foreseen, which is surprising with all the current advanced technology.

Ironically, speaking about space *colonies* or about exploring other planets doesn't bother or hurt those who are hostile to colonization. On the contrary, we praise the technological advancement of spaceships and the courage of those companies venturing on Earth's space, taking tourists to a short trip only affordable by the wealthiest, and aiming at populating (colonizing) other planets in the near future. Isn't this exactly what the colonizers of the 16th, 17th, and 18th centuries did? Aren't we doing exactly what we so furiously criticize? Shouldn't we hang on our principles, stay on our planet and leave the other ones alone? After all, it is not their fault if we are destroying our planet. Shouldn't we be against any kind of colonization?

The technological progress reached today doesn't seem to replace the natural human senses in identifying threats and opportunities. It is surprising that with real-time information and 4,550 satellites orbiting around the Earth, we can still be surprised with unforeseen events. Often the information is incomplete, misinterpreted, or even not used because people don't believe in it. So many human lives could have been saved from shootings and natural catastrophes if the people in charge of gathering the data, analyzing it, and propagating it were more rigorous and responsible. It looks like technology is only good for telling fictitious stories to all populations when it should be used to help all those populations to live in a better planet.

The main question, in this context, would be what do we want to become? Unified by one and same culture? Do we want to be supremacists over other species or races? Do we want to be people with no history? Or perhaps would we rather be genetically modified beings? Do we aim at being people with no religion or with the same religion to all? Same color of skin and same language to all? Or people with such polarized identities that we will no longer be able to live in the same place? Are we going back to the "purification" of races? Are we ready to accept technological colonization?

As stated by Harari (2015, 415), "seventy thousand years ago, Homo Sapiens was still an insignificant animal minding its own business in a corner of Africa. In the following millennia it transformed itself into the master of the entire planet and the terror of the ecosystem." Now it is leaning toward immortality. Yet, what we produced on Earth is not much of what we can be proud of. With all the progress we think we made, do we live better than 70,000 years ago? Is there less fighting? Is there less misery? Is there less suffering in the world? Will our greedy minds ever be satisfied with what we have today? We seem to be even more miserable now, when we witness violence, riots, protests, wars, murders, looting, and pandemics. As we claim human rights, we keep using children and women as slaves. We keep torturing animals and killing plants to build production plants. We poisoned our waters in such a way that it is dangerous to eat fish. We created useless summits to "save the planet" such as the Paris Accord while in 2021 Paris itself ranked as the fourth European city where people die because of air pollution and that the amount of CO_2 emissions among the countries having signed up to the COP 21 has significantly increased ever since (*The Lancet Planetary Health* in: *Le Monde* January 20, 2021).

Do we really know what we want and where we are going from here? Do we even have a goal for our existence? We might have no scientific answers to these questions. We might have intuitive answers to them. But one certainty is that we will keep living in a multicultural world and consequently we need to learn how to understand and respect cultural differences.

We are more and more dependent on communities. Never before had we feared as much as today to feel isolated. Long time ago, living in tribes was necessary for physical survival. Today we depend on communities for social survival. We belong to several communities at the same time as we seek for approval and validation. We consume products and brands that make us feel part of a community rather than those that we really need and make us feel good as an individual. Feeling good equals being accepted or, even better, being admired. Cultural communities are what make our world multicultural.

Implications for Multicultural Marketing

Taking culture for granted has been the main factor causing companies' failures in international settings. Marketers should know rather than assume. Often, they assume that some cultures are similar enough to accept the same globalized offer while it is assumed that some other ones would require adaptations in the marketing strategy. Marketers shouldn't yield to intuition; rather, they should study the cultures they are aiming at working with. Consumers around the world want to feel good through the consumption experience, but the "feel-good" sensation originated differently depending on the culture. Marketers should know what makes the difference.

Key Takeaways From Chapter 5

- Cultural intelligence is needed for a company to be successful in both multinational and multicultural settings.
- No purchase is ever totally rational.
- The use of emotions in marketing triggers interest and engagement from customers from all cultures.

CHAPTER 6

From Tribes to Virtual Communities

What's the Story?

Once upon a time, we believed in brands as being part of our personality and we gathered together with people who used the same brands, creating, this way, a brand community because people could relate to the story told by that brand, sometimes turning it into a myth. When advertising tells a credible story about a brand being the solution to customers' problems, consumers tend to believe it and buy that brand.

People consume because it makes them happy. Every time that something is missing or is not quite right, we buy a product or a service. Every time we feel bored with what we already have, we look for something else to consume, whether it is a new pair of shoes, or subscribe to yoga classes.

Consumers might never recognize it that way, or spell it out the same way, but they often show their new products with utmost pride to others. They buy certain brands to satisfy self-esteem needs and for self-expression purposes. For instance, when sporting luxury brands, consumers send a message of achievement to others. They tell a success story about themselves. They aim at conveying an image of sophistication, uniqueness, and belonging to a very selective group of people. Whether they do belong to that selective group or they just aspire to one day be accepted by its members, using such brands helps to build the image they want others to have of them as well as the image they want to have of themselves.

But some other customers will purchase specific brands because some influencer told them to do so. It doesn't seem to be reason enough to spend their money, but they proceed with the purchase without giving any additional thought to it. Consumers don't have the intellectual ability to explain emotional purchases. They have the transactional "need" of buying such a product and at the same time they have the emotional "want" to be part of the desired group of people they admire.

As the power of influencers grow and influencer marketing gains room and weight in companies, those who play the role of influencers are meant to play the intermediation role between companies and their clients. Customers might not recognize that they are influenced by advertising, but proudly disclose their following of some influencers and happily mimic their behavior. In an era where the new business models are the disintermediation, influencers become the intermediaries.

Disintermediation was supposed to bring closeness between the companies and their clients; yet, online shopping created a big disconnection with the human relationships in business. Social media gives people the feeling that they are involved in human relationships while their relationships are just virtual because they are filtered by the medium. Mediated communication is incomplete or partial as it violates the real relationship and creative communication people would have in-person. Yet, it gives the feeling that the world has no borders and people from around the world can be part of the same communities without living home.

In a "now" world created by technology, a company's success should not be based on how many products they were able to sell but on how many long-term relationships they were able to build across the years and across cultures. A company's capital is their relationship with their customers. Unlike relationships, products can be copied by competitors, whereas success comes from customer experience and loyalty because this is what makes companies profitable. A company is successful when their clients are loyal to them, purchase and promote the brand, and recognize their logo everywhere. Brands are the main asset companies have because customers are loyal to them, not to products.

Don't Worry; Be Happy!

Psychologist Iris Mauss and colleagues (2012) set out to investigate the unnerving paradox of pouring so much energy into being happy only to experience the opposite effect after noticing the demonstrative boom in self-help authors online and in bookstores. Happiness became a necessity and if you weren't happy then maybe you were following the wrong wellness coach. Happiness on its own should not be the marker of a life well-lived. The authors explain further how immersion in this new trend of how everyone should be focused on the pursuit of happiness at all times can often be a dubious one.

While pursuing happiness and a cheerful life are great goals, the obsession about them easily leads to disappointment. People tend to be disappointed in themselves when they realize that they are not as happy as they thought they should be. Often the lack of happiness is attributed to other people who were supposed to make them happy or who prevent them from being happy.

Happiness also rests on the ability of buying products, sporting famous brands, having a big social network, and collecting likes, shares, and followers in social media. But the opposite can lead to unhappiness and even to depression. Not being able to afford the trendy brands, being unsuccessful with the pictures posted on social media, or being criticized or, worse, being canceled has been causing the increase in suicide rates.

People have a hard time being alone and it has always been like that because humans are social beings. In the old times, when someone was banished from the tribe because of inappropriate behavior, they were physically isolated. Those who would not be strong enough to battle alone would starve to death. Those who would understand that they were on their own would keep hunting and survive. Today, it is the virtual isolation that is killing those who are not strong enough to understand that those people are not even part of their real lives and that they can easily keep living and being successful when relying on real people.

Life is full of triumphs and tribulations and a sober acceptance of this universal truth could bring some relief to many people. Yet, cases of depression have been increasing because when people are unhappy they think that their lives are not worthwhile. The covid years witnessed very high rates of suicide, the main reason being the human disconnection. As much as Zoom and Instagram are praised by everyone, what brought the numbers of suicide up was the lack of human contact. People felt isolated and their lives lost their meaning.

It is worth to note that the sources of happiness as well as the definition of happiness have no universal value. In some cultures, happiness comes from material possessions, while, in others, the source of happiness is the size of the family. Studies rating the happiest countries in the world have often pointed to poor countries as being the happiest ones in the world, where happiness is based on family gatherings around a frugal meal and a couple of beers. Same studies have demonstrated that the richer the people, the more stressed they are because they are haunted by the specter of losing what they possess. Thus, they invest part of their money in insurance and all kinds of security devices. And the more they have, the more they need to buy and worry. The more powerful and wealthier they are, the more they need bodyguards.

Those who have traveled outside of the top-tier rich countries have seen happiness in the eyes of people who would not even care about such possessions; the most important thing to them is being surrounded by family and friends—human connections is the key to their happiness. For no money in the world would they leave their country, their city, and their community because this is where they are happy. This is where they can trust people who will always be there for them whatever happens. There is solidarity, love, and genuine friendship. When they get together, their rule is "the more, the merrier." Everyone brings something to eat/drink, just like in a potluck; some play music and this is all they need to spend a cheerful Sunday together.

Sometimes happiness comes from the possession of pets. Thanks to their love for pets, humans have been devoting much time and spending much money on pet care. This one became a huge and promising market which goes way beyond selling food. There are treats (ice cream, bagels, cupcakes, etc.), specific for them, a broad range of branded clothes, with universities and sports teams' logos, shoes and boots, medals, toys, and so on. And because they ride with humans in their cars, sleep in their beds, rest in their couches, rugs, and carpets, several other products have been brought to the market, including pet hair fighter dryer sheets! Insurance companies didn't neglect this juicy market either. Medical care for pets can be very expensive and subscribing to insurance for them follows exactly the same rules as for humans at more or less the same price points.

Compliance Equals Peer Acceptance

The human mind is tuned to detect patterns, and meaningful patterns turn into stories in our minds. We belong to a community where people align their narratives with the narratives of other people around them. Religion creates communities because it provides multiple benefits to groups. Defined by Emile Durkheim (2011) as a unified system of beliefs and practices, religion unites into a single moral community those who adhere to them. Insofar, religion coordinates behavior within the group, setting up rules and norms, punishments and rewards. It also provides a powerful incentive system that promotes group cooperation and suppresses selfishness. The main function of religion, as for any other community, is to bind people together and make them put the group's interests ahead of their own (Wilson 2003). This priority of the group over self-interest is what enabled tribes to exist and survive.

Often criticized by atheists, religion establishes behavioral patterns of decency toward members of the group. As for any other community, these patterns can also create vigorous opposition to those who are not part of the same community. Religion is a critical cultural factor and it has initiated several wars. People born and raised in the same country would kill each other because of differences in religious beliefs. They feel like they don't belong to the same tribe. When one culture decides to take over others, it doesn't accept differences and doesn't acknowledge freedom of choice or of practices.

That is even more shocking today when tolerance, acceptance, and nondiscrimination are preached by politicians and media. Race communities, sex, and gender communities speak up and are expected to be accepted and respected by all other communities. Cultural communities are supposed to be respected too; unfortunately, this is not what happens. When there are diplomatic conflicts between countries, populations from these countries are brutalized and the brands from the same country are boycotted, which is totally irrational: populations and companies are not decision makers for these kinds of situations. The heads of states and only them are responsible for those conflicts.

Perhaps because real life is sometimes so disappointing, there is an exodus from the real to the virtual world as human attention is gradually switching to the virtual world. More than 20 hours per week are absorbed in online adventures and friendships are started with other players. The virtual world is becoming more and more attractive thanks to immersive technology and the compelling stories and adventures it provides as opposed to the unpleasant and repellent reality of the real world. Gamers can easily become what they want to be in the virtual world and interact with others who share the same interests as them. Virtual worlds are also a response to isolation in the real world. It gives a feeling of community and status in that community.

As a matter of fact, gamers, as a community, are a specific and growing target market for companies. Better yet, they seem to represent a unified community, sharing enough characteristics to accept standardized marketing products. Cultural adaptations to videogames might only rest on language translations because they are so fictitious that they can be used and understood everywhere. Videogames have the ability of telling stories around the avatar created by the gamers, which will be at the core of those stories. Indeed, gamers are the main characters in their stories.

Technology might have changed the way we communicate but has not destroyed the core role of storytelling since it has been orally conveyed to us for centuries. Story continues to fulfill its ancient function of binding society by reinforcing a set of common values and strengthening the ties within communities. It raises the youth and defines people. It teaches us to be decent rather than decadent because each story has a moral in its soul. Story is the glue of our society encouraging us to behave in a communal way by uniting people around common values.

Social media is successful because it is all about storytelling and it helps in creating the global village as predicted by McLuhan (1966). Technology has brought together widely dispersed people with the same media and made them citizens of a virtual village that spans the world. Stories are a low-cost source of information and enable others to live an experience through other people without the potential staggering costs of having to gain this experience firsthand. This gives them the false feeling that they know, but they don't. They live their lives through other people and repeat what they hear and read as if they have developed some expertise on the topic. And this is how misinformation is propagated and creates unrooted beliefs.

Entering fictional worlds radically alters the way information is processed. Green and Brock (2000) stated that the more absorbed we are in stories, the more they change us. Emotions of fiction are highly contagious and beliefs with consequent attitude change are more strongly impacted by fictitious communication than by nonfictitious communication. This explains why consumers tend to believe more in customers' reviews than in advertising. Even if they don't know whether the sources of those reviews are real customers, they will give more credibility to what doesn't come from the company.

Advertising Is Storytelling

Advertising is meant to inform and persuade consumers to choose specific products. To do so, advertisements demonstrate, through media, how much of a solution they are to consumers' problems. Most of the time, the story depicts the problematic situation consumers go through and the emergence of the product as being *the* solution to that situation.

Thus, if you don't have much time to clean, Swiffer makes it easier for you, and if your dog propagates smell in your home, Febreze is there to help you out with it, and so forth. Advertisers have very little room to tell a convincing story, because people zap, don't read, and just don't pay undivided attention to anything. Yet, if the story is incomplete, it is not understandable and is thus inefficient. It is a real challenge to captivate attention and tell a story with beginning, development, and conclusion to people who are not ready to listen to it.

Advertisements are stories we are told about products, brands, and companies. While enjoying the stories, most people don't like to admit that they are influenced by advertising (Becker et al. 2022). But they will happily spread the word about the products and brands they purchased thanks to influencers, tutorials, "independent experts," and reviews in social media. While they refuse to be "manipulated" by advertising, they believe in influencers because their celebrity is based on a story preceding the promotion they do of products. Their credibility also comes from the belief that these people are not part of the company so they are honest and uninterested. While consumers hate to be told that they are under the influence of advertising, they are proud to follow the directions given by influencers. Such influence is so powerful that "influencer" became a position, a profession, and a title. While "being under influence" was understood as a negative, pejorative, and dangerous situation, the word influencer has been redefined and presented in a positive way.

People buy less and less what they want and more and more what makes them "Insta-cool." If this is not shopping under influence, we'll need to find another word for it. People buy what they think they should buy to be accepted by the communities they belong or aspire to belong to. Such a community can be the one of followers of a specific influencer even if they will never meet the other followers. It is a virtual community. If the influencer is well known worldwide, the virtual community will be international, but if the influencer is only well known in the domestic market, the virtual community will be multicultural.

People consume because there is a promise of happiness. Those external stimuli trigger the flow of serotonin, dopamine, and oxytocin. Because opening a coke brings happiness and with Nike you can do it, consumers buy products in their endless quest for happiness. More so, they buy to comply with their tribes' rules. You need to buy the right brands to be accepted as a member of your tribe. Social pressure is much more powerful than advertising and, by extension, than marketing.

Often accused of lying, manipulating, and only showing the good sides of products, advertising is highly criticized by consumers. This is what we hear in surveys and marketing trainings. Then, I ask my participants what is it that they tell about themselves when they apply for a job: the good or the bad about themselves? And how much of a lie is in what they promise to the recruiters to get that job? This makes them realize that they are advertisers of their skills when they tell stories about themselves. A resume and a cover letter are stories about the applicants as are the subsequent interviews. People get dressed up (packaging), highlight their skills (product features), and discuss salary (price), while promoting their skills and contributions to the company. The same behavior relates to the start of a romantic relationship: only the good side is disclosed!

But as said before, stories are not one-sided. Stories are meant to give pleasure and instruction. They help create communities and define cultures. This is what global brands aim at through their advertising campaigns.

They promise that they will take you on a trip to their home country or even around the world. Most American companies were successful abroad because they would bring the "American Way of Life" so many people dreamed of in other countries. This dream was created and sustained by Hollywood productions such as movies, TV shows, and theme parks. They are all about storytelling.

Such productions would depict beautiful and wealthy people, heroes, success, achievement, adventure, romance, glamour, and fame. The stories are told in a very enticing way, transporting the viewers to other horizons with dreams which could come true thanks to the products brought by global companies they would now be able to enjoy. The stories told by global advertising are believed to address a cross-cultural target market, assuming that everyone has the same dreams and enjoy the same stories. This is particularly true to luxury brands.

Luxury brands tell stories that make people feel special and unique. Consumers might not pay an extra dollar for an advertised product deeming it "too expensive" but they happily use their credit cards to buy a branded product so that others can identify them as being part of that specific community. Inspired by their international and sometimes global reach, luxury brands adapt their stories to different countries and convey a message that better aligns with the local culture. In a research I conducted along with a colleague for a global advertising campaign for the French champagne brand Moët & Chandon across seven countries, we found out that they conveyed a different message by telling a different story to each country. Although champagne as a product category is positioned as being a product for celebrations, the story depicted different kinds of celebrations in each country.

Therefore, in France, the story would refer to roses just showing a bottle of a champagne rosé lying down on a rose (reference to the song "La vie en Rose" of Edith Piaf); in Italy, we would only see a woman with a bottle of champagne as for a lonely pleasure; and in the United States, the story is the glamour in the 1960's style depicting Scarlett Johansson with the same sensuality as Marilyn Monroe. In The Netherlands, celebration is represented by a table in a garden with two glasses of champagne, while in Germany, several situations of happiness are represented. Finally, in Japan, we see a party with only western-looking girls while in China, it is all about love and a romantic couple, referring to France as being the most romantic country in the world.

This analysis is indeed very interesting from the international marketing standpoint. But multicultural marketing is something else. Now let's imagine that consumers from all the cultures described earlier have migrated and live in the same foreign country, where the laws about advertising alcoholic beverages are different as are their reference systems when it comes to champagne as well as their perception of France. That would be confusing to some of the customers wondering what the company means by that story, what the message is about, and why they are allowed to show these kinds of pictures. While some companies think about adapting their communication to foreign countries, they always neglect the foreign cultures living in their own country.

The Storytelling Brand

Brands tell stories to consumers and about the consumers who display them. Brands, as a self-expression tool, are recognized by the logos sported by consumers. This is how they can display their belonging to a brand community in a more "subtle" way. Brand communities are constituted of very different people having only that brand name in common even if they might buy that brand for different reasons: aspiration to a group, quality of the products, country of origin of the brand, and the company, just to name a few.

The logo accompanying a brand name is a symbol and symbols are elements of culture loaded with cultural values and codes. Luxury brands often use luxury sports and powerful animals in their logos: polo, jaguar, horses, and so on. For some brands, logos are so well known that they got rid of the brand name; the vision of the logo alone enables consumers to identify the brand name. Not all consumers understand the logos or are aware of their stories, but they know which ones tell them what communities they should belong to.

Ironically, some consumers proudly wear t-shirts displaying brand names across their chests. When consumers behave this way, they dive deep in their own contradictions because they pay the company to advertise their brands. The explanation to such contradictions is the story consumers mean to tell about themselves: "I've been there" or "I can afford it," better yet, "I belong to this community."

Aspiration to be part of a specific community makes people buy specific brands. This is how brand communities are formed. Harley-Davidson and Apple know very well how to create and maintain their communities of consumers. These brands became such a myth that even people who can't afford a Harley motorcycle will at least buy their branded clothes or any other items with their logo. The same brand community applies to Ferrari. Yet, there are no advertisements for Ferrari or Harley-Davidson. But there is product placement, a much more powerful promotional tool.

In product placement, consumers see the brand playing a role in the plot; the brand is part of the story. Also, the brand can be associated with a character consumers admire and project themselves into, which makes it even more compelling. The mythic movie *Easy Rider* where Peter Fonda rides his Harley has strongly contributed to creating international brand awareness thanks to the access given to it through the film. With time, the number of loyal customers to the brand grew and ended up creating a brand community and the myth around the brand, which has been increasingly sustained by loyal customers of the brand around the world in such way that there is a specific club for Harley owners: the HOG. Other brands such as Starbucks have only very recently started to invest in advertising. The entire brand's communication rested on product placement in movies and TV shows, thanks to which the brand is recognized worldwide. Product placement instills a lifestyle to consumers from different cultures. When the brand reaches the foreign markets, there is already a latent demand for it generated by local consumers' exposure to the brand through movies and TV shows.

Brand Communities in the Multicultural Realm

Brands convey values and tell stories to consumers. It might be the story of the founders, which is often told as a sequence of successes, or in a more dramatic way, as very tough and uncertain beginnings to end up being one of the most valuable brands in the world. People get moved by those who started in a garage and turned simple ideas into financial empires. They become role models and inspire millions of people around the globe.

One excellent example of brand having built all their reputation on storytelling is the French perfume Chanel N°5. First, it is surprising that a product without a brand name could be so famous. After all, it is just a number signed by its creator, Coco Chanel. Yet, the mystery created about the number 5 has always attracted customers' attention. What is the meaning of that number? The story of this perfume tells that 5 was Chanel's favorite number and also the fifth scent proposed to her for this perfume. The glamour of the brand has been reinforced by the statement from Marilyn Monroe when she said that all she wore when going to sleep was two drops of Chanel N°5. The brand became so mythical that it inspired a painting from Andy Warhol and got exposed at the MOMA (Metropolitan Museum of Modern Art) in New York City. This is the story of the longevity of a product that has been successful across cultures for more than a century.

Coca-Cola is also an example of a brand being internationally consumed for more than 100 years. The story tells that it started in a pharmacy in Atlanta. But there has always been mystery about the use of cocaine among the ingredients and consumers around the world are hung up on this mystery. To add to the mystery, we are told that the recipe that makes all the success of Coke is secretly kept in a vault impossible to be violated.

Thanks to those (success) stories, these brands became myths. Myths disappeared as a literary genre and have been replaced by novels. But novels create myths through their characters and plots. Mythical brands tell stories about mythical businesses and founders, such as Steve Jobs, Elon Musk, and Jeff Bezos. Their companies wouldn't enjoy such an aura without them.

The book about Steve Jobs' life and the beginnings of Apple, which became a movie, was an international best seller mainly after he passed away. The value of the brand Tesla increases after each interview with the controversial Elon Musk and Jeff Bezos is considered the genius of the new business models with Amazon. Less promoted in media, yet not less well known and influential is Bill Gates, an entrepreneur having diversified his company in so many ways that he is at the highest levels of political influence in his country and abroad. Facebook, Google, and Starbucks have also well sold their books and movies showing how to pave the way to success.

While most of these mythic CEOs are American, we should remember that Elon Musk is South African and that Zoom's founder, Eric Yuan, is Chinese and that his brand turned into an international verb (Zooming) just like Google (Googling). In the same Hall of Fame is British Sir Richard Branson, founder and CEO of Virgin. Thanks to the diversification of his company (transportation, book stores, fitness clubs, food, etc.), his brand is well known worldwide and the fact that he has been knighted by Queen Elizabeth II adds to his aura. Last, but not least, in these examples is the Chinese Zhang Yiming, founder of TikTok, the most popular social media across cultures, yet less promoted than Jack Ma from Alibaba.

So many people dream of being as successful as those founders and CEOs, but how many of them really try to turn their dreams into reality? People believe in fiction and stories spread throughout social media, but don't believe in their most intimate stories which are their dreams. Sometimes, they don't even share their dreams with others because they are their secret dream and they are scared at being mocked because they know that they will keep them at the level of dreams. Those who dare turn their dreams into businesses work their way to success and persevere, but those who don't venture and just continue dreaming, the day they wake up their frustration hits them hard.

Brand positioning also comes from the founders' beliefs. Soichiro Honda said that "We all have the right to our crazy dreams," which explains the brand's tagline "Honda, the Power of Dreams." Often, brand loyalty comes from the admiration consumers have of the founder or of the brand's CEO. It is their personality that the brand incarnates and their pictures are worth much more than the brand's logo. Consumers have an emotional attachment to brands, and in many cases, this attachment comes from the aspiration to become as successful as those they consider as being their role models. People like success stories.

Everyone in the world is familiar with the names and photos of the founders of Google, Microsoft, Tesla, Amazon, and Facebook because they are often seen in the news and that technology is the hot contemporary topic. But much less is known about the companies providing the most basic products consumers need to live: food and clothes. No one knows the name of the founder of Coca-Cola Company or of those of

McDonald's. Yet, the two brands enjoy high rates of brand awareness. But because they are not recent and even less in the technology industry, consumers have less interest in knowing more about them. Also, as they have been around for so long, customers just take them for granted; they are just places they go to everyday. There is no much excitement about that. Luxury brands also have books and movies to tell their stories such as Chanel and Gucci. Consumers not being able to afford these brands can still be, in some measure, part of their stories when watching the movies and knowing more about the brands.

Brands would have no value without the stories they convey to consumers. These stories create a strong relationship with the customer and the subsequent customer loyalty. It is notorious that loyal customers are the most profitable ones not only because they increase the company's turnover in terms of sales but also because a bad customer service can cause losses up to 76 percent. Loyal customers become brand ambassadors and refer other customers to the brand. And this is how the brand communities are created and sustained.

A good example of brand community-based stories is Crumbl Cookies. Thanks to their positioning in bringing innovative flavors for their cookies every week, they created a brand community of loyal customers who meet on TikTok every week to share their pictures and speak about the new cookies they've sampled. In doing so, each customer shares their stories with these cookies: which ones, where, with whom they consumed their cookies, and how much they recommend them. The advantages are threefold: loyalty from consumers, increase of brand awareness, and brand appropriation through personal stories—all of that free of charge for the company!

What a person wears in public speaks for their success represented by the price of specific brands, individuality that is expressed by the designs they choose, and inclusion into specific groups. Most premium sneakers represent an artist, musician, athlete, or influencer through collaborations. Therefore, wearing these shoes provides the consumers with the feeling that they are part of these collaborations. For example, one of the most valued Nike shoes are the Air Jordans, and customers are willing to pay the price for them. Such loyalty to the brand originated in emotional storytelling. When NBA banned Nike shoes because of lack of conformity with their rules, Nike undertook a communication campaign inviting everybody to use them to feel like a champion (Just do it). It is a story of turning a ban into a marketing opportunity. Customers felt like they were supporting Michael Jordan more than the brand. The story brought U.S.$100 million to Nike in 1985. Up until today, Jordan's shoes are still profitable weighting U.S.$5 billion (this figure will certainly go up with the release of the movie telling Jordan's life's story) and the brand keeps capitalizing on athletes' stories such as Kevin Durand (Nike KD) and Kyrie Irving (Kyrie's).

Wearing shoes with athletes' signatures not only addresses self-expression needs but also self-satisfaction ones, which relate to self-actualization needs as per Maslow's classification of human needs. It feels good to "look" like successful people and consumers project themselves on those they admire.

That is why cobranding is a marketing practice that entices consumers at the highest levels. Cobranding rests on the agreement of two brands to sign with both their brands a new line of products addressing the same target market. Nike has been cobranding with Coke in creating a line of polo shirts and shoes while Pepsi did the same with Puma. This way, companies cater to customer loyalty from both sides: to the beverage and to the sports' brand.

The existence of brand communities is nothing new. What is new is the ability of social media in creating and maintaining such communities. The magic of online communities is that people willingly belong to several communities simultaneously and interact with people from around the world without never getting to know them in person. Fans from all cultures are brought together by the brand alone. This might be the only thing they have in common and it is a witness of the power of brand loyalty. Brand communities have no borders and they are multicultural because people from different cultures purchase the same brand. But their only common point is their interest in the brand and that is why they are a community and not a culture. Unlike cultures, communities are rootless.

Brands tell their followers to post pictures of themselves when using their brands. Not only selfies but having pictures of friends wearing the same brand is already halfway to creating a community. Converse does it very well as does GoPro with the impressive high-quality photos and videos users can take when practicing any sport. Consumers might purchase this brand because of the high quality of its products, but the main motivation is to be able to take their own pictures and videos when they are biking, surfing, and bridge jumping and easily share them with the brand community and with all the other virtual communities they belong to. The brand invites them to "be heroes of their lives" and this is the story they share on social media. Being part of virtual communities is such a vital endeavor today that people even die taking selfies in very dangerous places. They will risk their lives to impress people they don't even know and will most certainly never meet in person. This is the pressure exerted by compliance.

One brand to be admired in creating closeness with their consumers is Oreo. The brand celebrates every single date: Valentine's, Christmas, Easter, Pride month, July 4, Halloween, birthdays—all with new products and packaging especially created for those events. Thanks to the widespread use of promotional practices, recipes of desserts made out of Oreos proliferate on social media. Countless videos posted by consumers on YouTube and on TikTok disclose all kinds of desserts possible to be made with this simple cookie. Consumers are the best endorsers of the brand. They show their creativity and tell the story of the recipes they created all with joy and good humor, just like the brand tells them to be: "Stay Playful!"

Another noteworthy example is Patagonia. The company produces and sells outdoor clothing and gear but by having a unique positioning they created a brand community across cultures bringing together people who believe in activism for saving the planet. As a matter of fact, their mission went from building "the best product, cause no unnecessary harm, use business to inspire and implement solutions to the environmental crisis" to "We're in business to save our home planet." They define their business as being the climate crisis and link sports with activism. Customers are invited to explore activism stories, to connect with environmental groups in order to discover the most pressing stories from environmental protectors across the world, and get inspired. In other words, the brand is campaigning to bring political or social change. We can say that the brand addresses a universal target, because there are customers concerned about the planet and climate change in all cultures, and among those, the ones who can afford Patagonia's high-end products. The brand community is brought together by activism in favor of the planet.

Another example of universal target serving people from all cultures thanks to brand community is DUDEWipes. This company from Chicago, created in 2011, sells "Flushable *wipes* for on-the-go and at home shituations." By addressing men in this basic human need, the brand community spans cultures by creating a product that is specific to this demographic. Their customers share their stories online expressing their difficulties with other (Baby) wipes and how satisfied they are with DUDEWipes. The success of the company came from their deep understanding, solidarity, and empathy with those the founders know well and is now diversifying their lines of products into other toilet-related solutions.

People Invest in Relationships

As easy as it might seem to become the member of a community, it is worth noting that to be a member of a community, it is imperative to comply with their rules, traditions, rituals, and behaviors. There are standards that should be observed by all members or the punishment will be exclusion. This is the foundation of cancel culture: members of a community canceling their fellow members or members from other communities because they don't agree with what they stand for.

Unlike tribal times when expelling someone was decided by a group of sages who would judge the seriousness of the misconduct by that member, in social media, anyone, without such authority but self-granting themselves such power, can start a canceling movement against literally anyone. There are no more boundaries among the communities when it comes to cancel culture. Without social media, this kind of interference would have never been possible, and those intending to cancel anyone from outside their community would have been invited to mind their own businesses.

This is made even clearer when it comes to international business and diplomacy. Whenever countries or foreign companies go abroad and criticize the local rules and try to change them, two possible consequences are to be considered: the local market complies because they need that investment or protection very badly or they send the foreigners back home. Whichever the time in history and the kind of tool used to accept or reject members in a society, compliance remains the golden rule to be part of a community.

Members of a community have one or more interests in common but they don't have the same cultural roots, unless it is a cultural community. Most communities such as brand communities or gamers' communities span cultures and that is why they are multicultural. As we live in a multicultural world and most of the communities are multicultural, cultural diversity needs to be understood and incorporated in marketing decisions.

Tiesta Tea understood how to create a community in using the trendy social interests of contemporary consumers. The company created an elegant recyclable aluminum packaging for their teas, with a vertical window through which the loose tea leaves can be seen. They created lines of products with compelling names such as Eternity, Immunity, Energizer, Slenderizer, and Relaxer within which they launched several products with appealing names such as Victorian Earl Grey, Passion Berry Jolt, Pineapple Blues, Lean Green Machine, Maui Mango, and Nutty Almond Cream. Other than these amusing names, they bring their consumers together thanks to their promise of sourcing only premium ingredients from across the globe and never using anything artificial and donating directly back to the global, national, and local communities who support them. This is how the company entices their consumers without a big promotional budget.

With the pervasive role played by technology, social media grew exponentially in few years and brands seized the opportunity of addressing virtual communities. They replaced their marketing efforts previously invested in traditional media, with social media, some companies even operating 100 percent virtually. Interestingly, these same companies are now using traditional media to promote their products and expand their target markets. There are now TV commercials for TikTok, WhatsApp, Airbnb, Meta, and so on. These companies finally realized that they limited their customer base when using always the same communication channels. To corroborate this new trend, a study published in the *Harvard Business Review* (2022) states that traditional advertising will grow 2.9 percent in 2023 that services to consumers will increase their TV commercials' budget of +10.2 percent, and goods to consumers will grow +4.9 percent in advertising spent. The study outcomes add that companies who earn 100 percent of their sales through Internet will see +11.7 percent increase in traditional advertising spent.

The article also highlights that traditional media is more efficient to build brand trust thanks to the trust in traditional advertising; 82 percent of consumers rely on print advertising, 80 percent on TV, 76 percent on direct mail, and 71 percent on radio to make purchase decisions.

It is a plausible assumption that with less investment from companies, virtual communities might also weaken leading consumers to create new channels for interactions and belonging. As a matter of fact, the role of influencers is already decreasing in some countries because companies are investing back in traditional media: influencers became too expensive and difficult to control. In addition, the more consumers realize that some influencers are paid by the brands, the less they are credible and thus lose most part of their followers. This will unavoidably lead to the disruption of virtual communities created around influencers.

This is the consequence of too much use of the same communication method. An old Chinese saying states that "an excess of light blinds the human eye, an excess of noise ruins the ear and an excess of condiment deadens the taste" (Goddard 2022). This means that when everyone does the same thing, that thing loses its authenticity and consequently loses its attractiveness and power very easily.

In a world dominated by self-promotion, the interest in who people are is yielding to mediocrity. All communication is focused on self-expression with little content and depth. Returning to the roots is seeking tranquility by better understanding oneself. This partially explains why children of immigrants are always curious about their parents' home countries and aim at visiting or even moving back there in order to reconnect with their deepest cultural roots. The explanation is that the parents promote their home culture spontaneously because they miss it and they make their story credible because they are sincere.

Implications for Multicultural Marketing

Just like cultural communities, brand communities gather people who believe in the power of a brand in making their lives better. When they buy luxury brands, they feel good because they belong to a group they aspire to. Self-satisfaction and self-expression are drivers of consumer behavior, which can be achieved with not only global brands but also local brands. In some countries, pride is generated by purchasing local brands while in some others, international brands are more fulfilling. Multicultural marketers should understand the specific meaning of foreign brands in specific product categories and cultures.

Key Takeaways From Chapter 6

- Brand communities establish patterns of consumption and behavior.
- A persuasive story is the one that presents solutions to a problem.
- Brand communities rest in relationships both at the consumer-to-consumer (C2C) and consumer-to-business (C2B) levels.

CHAPTER 7

Cultural Diversity Is the Path to Growth

What's the Story?

Once upon a time, people got confused with similar yet different concepts. Diversity became synonymous with inclusion and minorities. Culture was confounded with community, nation, and race; and universalism and unity became interchangeable terms. It was time to well-define those terms to understand how crucial openness to diversity is to both multicultural and multinational marketing.

The term diversity has never been this trendy although it is not a new one. But currently, and with the support of media and social media, the term has been mistakenly implying the predominance of racial minorities in a given population. In reality, the term diversity implies a representation of the whole array (diversity, kinds, types) of people existing in a society, not only minorities. Diversity includes races, cultures, genders, professions, talents, ages, and any other skills and characteristics describing a given population. This is what makes diversity interesting.

Being open to diversity means being curious about others and willing to learn from them. And that is independent of race. Race being biological, it doesn't tell much about you. All you can know about someone, based on their race, is the color of their skin, the shape of their eyes, and their height, which they inherited from their parents. It is impossible to get acquainted with their ideas, values, lifestyle, and language, because none of these have to do with race.

It is also imperative to understand the main differences between culture and community. There are several cultures within one community. For instance, vegetarians are a community, and people from different cultural backgrounds join that community because they are vegetarians. The same applies to the vegan and LGBTQ+ communities. People belonging to these communities don't even speak the same language. When it comes to the black community, which has been mistakenly called black culture, we should think about the black population in the most multicultural continent in the world: Africa. There are around one billion black inhabitants in the African continent and they span 54 countries. Those countries speak different languages and have different historical roots, different religious beliefs, different rituals, and so on. Briefly said, they are all culturally different and those having emigrated to other countries brought with them their own respective cultures, just like any other immigrants. In addition, around 10 billion people in the world belong to the black race. Knowing that there are around 200 countries in the world, the black population spans that many different cultures. For this reason, speaking about black culture is inaccurate.

Once I said in a course that race could not be a culture and one of my students got hurt in his beliefs because he was referring to the black culture. Although he could understand my scientific and conceptual explanations, emotionally he could not accept that the stories ingrained in his education could be false. Then I asked him the following question: if I were to describe you to someone who doesn't know you, what would you rather have me to say about you: my student is black or my student is bright, pertinent, kind, a great team player, and a real added value to the class? He agreed that defining him as belonging to a race didn't tell much or anything about him. I would have defined him even better if he knew his cultural roots, but he didn't. All he knew was that he should be proud of being black because that one was his culture. Just like for this student, there are millions of people unable to understand that they are being lured with stories based on inaccurate definitions. When you see some TV programs announcing a show "for the culture about the culture" while it is about a specific race, it is easy to understand why the wrong word is spread out so quickly. TV shows also promote the black experience and the black excellence. This is hard to understand. It would be more appropriate to speak about the Ethiopian delicious food experience, the Nigerian film excellence, or the Jamaican reggae rhythm. Not all the cultures involving black populations have the same talents and offer the same experience.

There are several cultures in the black community, such as Ghanaian, Nigerian, Togolese, and Camrounese, and they are all culturally different. Same applies to all races. Defining someone as black, white, Asian, or Latinx not only doesn't tell much about them but is also and mainly disrespectful. Limiting a person to their physical features is removing everything that the person stands for. Their values, skills, background, and accomplishments are ignored as if they were unimportant. In addition, it places all people of the same race at the same level, which we all know is not accurate. Black populations have been defined by others, by the color of their skin and rejected because of that for more than two centuries. Now, that the black population enjoys respect and equality, they are defining themselves the same way, by the color of their skin what ultimately is not really a sign of evolution.

A community can't be a culture either because all that their members share is one common interest. Pet owners, smokers, gamers, gamblers, and parents are examples of communities. Some of them are real (we might know some parents from our children's school), but most of them are imaginary communities because they are constituted of people we don't know, will never know, and don't even know how many and where they are. The need for belonging is so powerful that it makes us imagine that millions of strangers are part of the same community. And that we have common interests and a common future with them! These communities exist because we are drawn to believe that they can exist. We are told beautiful and sad stories about people around the world we have nothing to do with but with whom we are supposed to identify because we belong to the same sex, gender, race, hobby, and so on.

Instead, people belonging to the same culture share deep-rooted values because they also have a shared history, geography, norms, language, and other capabilities enabling them to be members of that specific society. They were raised with such values and norms.

As a matter of fact, what makes you who you are is your culture, not your race. Your physical appearance is a biological heritage from your parents. Yet, your culture might be rooted in your parents' culture, but you build your own as you grow up and get to know other cultures. Unlike race, culture is not innate; it is learned. When we are exposed to other cultures, we learn from them and we adapt ourselves to them, whereas we carry our innate race forever. Our culture evolves as we travel and get to know people from other cultures, while we belong to the same race until we die.

We don't choose our race nor do we choose our parents' culture or the culture we are socialized in. But we can choose the culture we want to be part of when we are of age. We can also change our physical appearance if we don't like the way we look, but we'll keep belonging to the same race forever. What makes us "us" are the choices we make which pave the way to our accomplishments and to whom we want to be.

Focusing all the stories on racial differences is very convenient if we aim at pushing people against each other. As a matter of fact, race being physically visible, it makes it easier to identify different people and automatically reject them, while accepting those who look alike, whereas it is impossible to identify one's culture without speaking with them. Thus, we can see who looks Asian, black, white, and Hispanic, without knowing their culture. This is one of the reasons why multiracialism is taking over multiculturalism. We are encouraged to remain within our racial communities rather than discover other cultures across communities. Yet, it could be a good surprise to see how much people from different cultures can have something in common. As different as cultures can be, there are always similarities across them. In addition, there is much more in people than race and culture: people have personalities, lifestyles, preferences, and similar life and family experiences that can relate to people from around the world, independently of their race and culture.

If we are happy to get to know different people, and we are curious about those who are different from us, we are open to diversity, but if we choose to live only among ourselves, then we don't enjoy diversity. Multiculturalism is the diversity of cultures, not of races. The world is multicultural, and it is an individual decision to know how much of this multiculturalism we want to soak up. The same applies to sex and gender. Sex is biological: we are born male or female. Gender is a social construct.

The world needs diversity in flora and fauna. We are part of the animals populating this world and more than ever, we are encouraged to respect nature. People are part of nature and they should participate in the protection of all species. We also need to protect multiculturalism. It is not good news when a culture takes precedence over others and is proud of doing so. Cultural imperialism is the opposite of multiculturalism. Cultures are different; they are neither better nor worse, neither superior nor inferior, just different, and this is the beauty of multiculturalism.

Culture Is a Survival Kit

Culture has been defined as the capabilities learned by people to be a member of a society. And because each society has its own shared values, cultures are different and require specific behavioral patterns. In multicultural settings, people from different cultural backgrounds abide by the same general rules when immersed in the prevalent culture, but observe specific rules when they are back in their native cultures. In countries well known as being multicultural, the population is composed of several different cultural backgrounds generated by immigration.

Immigrants tend to create their own communities as they tend to live in the same neighborhoods. Thus, they create mini replicas of their home cultures. They create their own cultural microenvironment in their neighborhoods with restaurants, shops, religious temples, museums, and sometimes their own schools aiming at recreating the same cultural context they left behind. The first generations of immigrants don't speak the local language very well but make the needed effort to acculturate to the host culture fearing rejection. Their children, however, are born in the host country and assimilated to the host culture. Therefore, they are bicultural because they are raised with their parents' original cultural values while embracing the local culture when interacting with natives of the host culture both at school and at the workplace. Thus, they speak one language at work and another one at home. They comply with the host country's rules when they are outside of their neighborhood but fit in their parents' culture when they are back home. This is how countries become multicultural—through the integration of different cultures in their own country.

In addition, children of immigrants are raised with the stories told by their family members. Such stories are filled with nostalgia of the country they grew up in, happiness in remembering their youth with their friends and families, and sadness because of wars and the loss of friends and family members and for having left their country behind. This is how the heroes of their families become their children's heroes and the enemies of their families become their own enemies even if they will never meet them for real. Stories can convey both admiration and hatred. Depending on how the immigration process is narrated by the parents, their children will either admire and respect the host country for having welcomed their parents or hate it and look for revenge if their parents suffered while settling in the foreign country.

The stories are also built on the practice of specific rituals celebrating key dates of the immigrants' home countries' history. Folklore, arts, language, and food are all part of building a culture within a culture. And they all tell stories about that specific culture. The survival of any culture is dependent on the transmission of cultural values through stories conveyed from one generation to the next.

A multicultural country celebrates all of these rituals and welcomes different practices and lifestyles, without stigmatizing any of them. Indeed, the Chinese New Year is celebrated outside of China in countries where there is a Chinese community. The same applies to Christmas in countries where there is a Christian community, Greek Easter outside of Greece, 5 de Mayo outside of Mexico, July 14th outside of France, Saint Patrick's outside of Ireland, and July 4th outside of the United States. Those celebrations are sometimes limited to the specific cultural community and sometimes widespread across the countries where people from other cultures join in.

Usually, we don't celebrate the same rituals because we are unfamiliar with the stories having originated them, and thus they don't make sense to us unless we are told a convincing story about them. This would include the rituals celebrated by people from other cultures without any understanding of cultural roots, just because everybody is doing it; we join in because it is trendy. For instance, more and more people celebrate the Chinese New Year and look for their signs in the Chinese zodiac without being Chinese or even being aware of the roots of such celebrations.

Along with cultural diversity come not only rituals and celebrations, but also new myths and superstitions. The Celtic festival known as Samhain celebrated the belief that on that day, the souls of the dead returned to their homes, so people dressed in costumes and lit bonfires to ward off spirits. Today, the ritual of Halloween has gained several other countries. The same "cultural contamination" relates to superstitions with numbers such as 13 originated by the Christian beliefs or the Chinese death number 4.

Multiculturalism started in some countries long before massive immigration. The United States, for example, was populated by several culturally different Native American tribes. They were physically different, spoke different languages, lived in different parts of the country, ate different food, celebrated different rituals, and had different superstitions and myths. Today, the country is even more multicultural thanks to immigration and it is home to more than 200 cultures coming from all continents in the world with 50 million foreign-born residents.

The United States has always been multicultural and a role model of multiculturalism. Today, rather than leading the world toward the understanding of the benefits and the richness of multiculturalism, the country is falling backwards in turning multiculturalism into multiracialism.

Openness to Diversity

Multicultural minds understand that there is no such thing as right or wrong in culture; there are only differences and they are beneficial to everyone. If anything, those differences increase knowledge and make all cultures more dynamic and interesting. Thereby, it would be expected that those populations are more open to diversity.

Concerned about cultural integration of students in college, some researchers created a scale to measure their openness to diversity.

The Openness to Diversity and Challenge (ODC) scale was created by Pascarella and colleagues in 1996 for the National Survey of Student Learning. The scale included eight items concerned with students' openness to diverse cultures, races, ethnicities, and values as well as individuals' willingness and enjoyment of having their ideas challenged by different values and perspectives. Enrollment in diversity-related courses, discussing controversial topics that challenged students' perspectives, interactions with diverse peers, a positive campus climate, climate for diversity, and living on campus were all associated with students' increased ODC at the end of the first year of college.

As such, openness to diversity is often measured using a 5-point Likert scale including statements such as (a) I believe contact with individuals whose backgrounds (race, national origin, sexual orientation) differ from my own is an essential part of my college education; (b) I enjoy taking courses that challenge my beliefs and values; (c) I most enjoy the courses that make me think about things from a different perspective; (d) I believe that learning about people from different cultures is a very important part of my college education; (e) I enjoy having discussions with people whose ideas and values are different from my own; (f) I enjoy talking with people who have values different from mine because it helps me better understand myself and values; and (g) I agree that the real value of a college education lies in being introduced to different values.

Aiming at measuring the validity of the ODC scale after more than two decades, I conducted a research with graduate students in a major diverse university in the United States. The first phase of the study was purely observational and involved a group of 24 graduate students enrolled in an elective multicultural marketing course in 2019. The second observation was conducted with the same course in 2020 and counted 22 graduate students. Students' behavior was observed when they were required to freely choose any ethnic community they would like to study. I assumed that if they were open to diversity, they would seize the opportunity to figure out an unfamiliar ethnicity; if they were not open to diversity, they would stick with their own cultural communities. The latter happened; the vast majority of students chose their own communities to study rather than taking the opportunity to get to know cultures they were unfamiliar with. The lesson to learn from these findings is that living and working in a multicultural environment doesn't make people more open to diversity. Even bicultural students, who could have been more sensitive to multiculturalism and thus more open to other cultures, remained within their cultures of origin (Karsaklian 2020).

To corroborate these findings, a student of mine recently conducted extensive research in bringing together the most widespread frameworks of cultural analysis, personality traits, and the ODC scale. Her methodology incorporated observation and interviews with respondents from 18 to 63 years old from more than 15 different cultural backgrounds. Her findings demonstrated that people from countries categorized as being individualistic in Hofstede's framework (the framework is extensively explained in Chapter 8) were more open to diversity than those from collective cultures. As counter intuitive as these results could seem to be, they reinforce the idea that the more collective people are, the more they tend to reject people who don't belong to their community. Findings also showed that the younger the respondents the less open to meeting different people they are (Karsaklian 2021). They would stick together with those who were like them. As a matter of fact, during the observation phase, it was noticed that students will gather with people with the same cultural and/or racial background.

These findings might come as a surprise in a world where everything promoted by the media is how people, mainly the younger generations, are tolerant, open to diversity, and fight for equal rights, when research shows that, in real life, people would rather stick together within their own communities and reject all those who are not like them. The main takeaway is that there is always a gap between the stories people tell and what they do. Among people who claim equal rights and the end of segregation are those who segregate by rejecting all those who don't belong to their community.

This gap between stories (discourse) and actions (behavior) can also be explained by the comfort people feel when being in familiar settings and the social desirability bias. Social convention dictates to say that they accept differences by fear of rejection or of a backlash, but they know that they don't feel comfortable around people different from them.

Social pressure imposes a ready-to-use story to everyone today: tolerance, acceptance, and equality. Yet, we know that we can't expect every human being to enjoy or even accept differences. It is just part of the human nature. Some are more open; some are less. And this is independent of race, culture, or gender. What they really are and believe in is reflected in human behavior rather than in their narratives. With the narrative of globalization, we make people think that everybody accepts everybody and that thanks to globalization we are all the same. Such narrative enables us to criticize countries that don't share the same mainstream values, which is absurd, because values are deep rooted in history, religion, geography, and everything else that constitutes a culture. And that is why cultures are different as are mindsets.

Admittedly, a global culture would make marketers' lives much easier—no need of adaptations—however, less interesting to all of us.

But global culture is more of an illusion than a possibility because global cultures are rootless and memory less. Brand communities seem to represent global cultures, but such cultures are created and sustained by the brands' communication. As explained before, the only thing people using the same brand have in common is that brand. Otherwise, they are all culturally different.

Beyond Race

We belong to the same species (*sapiens*) but to different cultures. And sometimes we belong to the same race but to different cultures.

Every culture has a cultural scheme that is an extension of the biological scheme. The biological schemes identify a need and the cultural scheme interprets it within the parameters of a particular culture. Biological schemes are specific to each species and are not negotiable. Thereby, life is tension and everything we experience in life lies somewhere between two extremes. Just like culture, the human body is an ecosystem in constant struggle and adaptation: good bacteria versus bad bacteria; reactions to foods and drinks, to tobacco and drugs, to internal versus external temperatures; and so on. Biology enables a vast array of possibilities which are only restricted by culture. Culture, through people, decides what is natural and unnatural. From the biological point of view, whatever is possible is natural.

But to make happen what seems to be impossible, humans created myths and fictions. They accustom people to think in certain ways, to behave in accordance with certain standards, to want certain things, and to observe certain rules. Since their birth, people are included in this mass of artificial instincts that enable millions of strangers to cooperate effectively. This network of artificial instincts can be called cultural norms.

As stated by Harari (2015, 161),

> during the first half of the twentieth century, scholars taught that every culture was complete and harmonious, possessing an unchanging essence that defined it for all time. Each human group had its own world view and system of social, legal and political arrangements that ran as smoothly as the planets going around the sun.

In this view, cultures did not change unless there was a force coming from outside. We know today that this is not true and that cultures have specific and different beliefs, norms, and values, but these are in constant flux. Unlike the laws of physics, which are universal, everything created by humans is made of contradictions and cultures are constantly trying to reconcile these contradictions and this process fosters change.

Some cultures display this contradiction in their most fundamental values. The French always claim equality, fraternity, and freedom as the fundamental values of the French republic. Yet, individual freedom and equality are opposed values because each individual freedom is cramped by equality. If every individual would be free to do as they wish, there wouldn't be equality. Individual freedom can only be limited to individuals being part of any society because all of them are expected to comply with general rules on behalf of equality and justice, not mentioning the cancel culture practiced in the so-called democratic countries, where the freedom of speech and of opinion only apply to those who reinforce the mainstream story. Fairness comes from having respect for people by taking them just as what they are: people, independently of their race, sex, gender, and culture. Everyone is entitled to be respected.

A word in vogue today is "authenticity." People want what is authentic. But what does it really mean? If it means purity, that is, without external influences, then there are no authentic cultures in the world as there are no pure races either. No human being develops independently, neither do cultures nor races. All our roots are in past interactions with other peoples and other cultures. One of my students used to say that she was Mexican because she indeed was born and raised in Mexico. One day, she decided to know more about her cultural roots and purchased the services of these companies that track peoples' genealogy. She learned that she was only 5 percent Mexican and that her ancestors had been in interactions with several other cultures. It was a very disturbing discovery to her because she had been raised as a monocultural and monoracial person. If people were not interested in knowing about their culture, these companies would be out of business because we don't need to go this far to know about our race.

The example above describes the difference between citizenship and culture. In reality, that student of mine owned the Mexican citizenship, but she had multicultural roots. Nationality can be determined by the country you were born in thanks to the birthright citizenship law. That is why in some countries, what counts is not the territory but the blood (law of blood): children inherit their parents' citizenship and culture rather than the birth country's one. Indeed, the country you land in when you are born doesn't define your culture. What does define your culture is the country you are raised in along with your parents' culture.

This way, the United States segments its multicultural population as African Americans, Asian Americans, Hispanic Americans, and Caucasian Americans, the designations implying biculturalism. This means, these people are Americans because they were born in the United States (birthright citizenship), but their cultural roots are abroad. Yet, this is not enough to define their cultures because their roots are in different countries in Africa and Asia, as well as in different Hispanic and Caucasian countries. Only the Native Americans are deep rooted in the same territory.

Multiculturalism also implies ethnic cuisine, which has been attracting people's preferences around the world because it is supposed to reflect the "authentic" cuisine of countries around the world. If you expect to eat that delicious "authentic" tomato sauce in an Italian restaurant, you should first know that tomatoes are Mexican in origin and reached Europe only after Spaniards conquered Mexico. Italians may have created their own authentic sauce out of tomatoes, but there is nothing "authentic" about the use of tomatoes by Italians. Potatoes arrived in Poland 400 years ago and the steaks we can eat in the American continent started in 1492 when Europeans arrived there. The same applies to the Australian steaks. And the glamorous Swiss chocolate comes from either Mexican or African cocoa beans. Likewise, Godiva, the famous Belgian chocolate brand sold around the world, has their chocolate made of beans from Congo.

We might fight injustices committed centuries ago, but we forget that who we are today is a consequence of what our cultures went through. If we enjoy technology, traveling, learning other languages, our material possessions, and comfort, while fighting our past, we forget that the past shapes the future and not the other way around, with all its bad and good. And the myths we create today through the stories we tell our children will shape their future.

There is always this temptation of depicting history in a binary way: good guys and bad guys. Of course, the empires are always depicted as having been the bad guys. But wars didn't start with colonialism. Rival tribes would fight each other for territory and power ever since the beginning of humankind. Neanderthals disappeared from earth because *sapiens* exterminated them. We are *sapiens* and we exterminated a whole species. How should we pay for our crime today?

Thus, we are the fruit of our colonization. If they were bad, we are bad. Yet, we find imperial legacies in the majority of modern cultures. Most people think and speak in imperial languages that were forced upon our ancestors by the sword. Why do we keep using them so many centuries later? We are no longer forced by the sword. This means, we think that the legacy is not all bad and we are happy to accept part of it while fighting them for what we are not happy to accept because it goes against the contemporary patterns of thought.

Some cultural legacies are not rejected and are even praised; Australia, New Zealand, India, and Pakistan are among the best cricket teams in the world, along with England, their colonizer. The same applies to Rugby. From this point of view, these countries don't reject their historical heritage and are proud to display their superior performance in these sports. Even if Australia created their own football rules—the Aussie Rules—they are very much into cricket and rugby. And they all drive on the left side of the road!

The Unification of the Humankind Is an Economic Process

With the development of international trade came the idea of a universal (global) order governing the entire world. All animals live in tribes and don't care about their whole species, and so do *sapiens*. Despite the world's globalization, *sapiens* claim their closest interests, be it at the individual, race, or country's level. We might try to impose the same rules to everyone, yet people will do what is more favorable to the closer groups they belong to. All the movements in favor of a race or gender are based on individual interests. Not all women care about all women. If all these movements and demonstrations in favor of women were done on behalf of all their sex, women would stop employing women as their slaves in several countries or earning money by selling and renting other women to men's sexual satisfaction thereby using women prostitution to earn money. The same applies to races and cultures. People defend and protect their own close communities rather than their race or culture.

Unification comes from money. It came from gold when Europeans showed its value to the civilizations they conquered. Thus, the appearance of a single transnational and transcultural monetary zone led to the unification of the entire globe into a single economic and political sphere. People continued to speak different languages, believed in different Gods, and practiced different rituals but they all believed in gold as their common currency. Without this shared belief, global trading networks wouldn't have been possible. Today's international trade practices are a legacy of that time. The U.S. dollar is the currency used for international trades and the European Union imposes the same currency, the Euro, to the 19 members of the Eurozone, despite the cultural and economic discrepancies among those countries.

Money bridges cultural gaps and enables strangers to cooperate effectively. To do so, money needs universal trust and the trust in the self-regulatory forces of the markets: supply and demand. With money and trade come contracts and people believe in contracts, not in people. It is the only way to cooperate with strangers. And perhaps they are even less trustworthy when they live far away, speak a different language, practice different rituals, and don't believe in the same God. It is safer to trust a piece of paper signed by all parties.

The existence of long contracts with tough terms for penalties in case of lack of goodwill is material proof that the unification of cultures doesn't exist and that it will never happen. Unification implies consensus: everyone should have the same opinion about the same things, which is impossible among humans, let alone in a multicultural world.

Since around 200 BC, most humans have lived in empires and it seems likely that in the future too, most humans will live in one: in a global empire. More and more people believe that all of humankind is the legitimate source of political authority, rather than the members of a particular nationality, and that safeguarding human rights and protecting the interests of the entire human species should be the guiding light of politics. This means, all nations are expected to free up all their regulations and independence to follow strictly the same rules from a higher global power and this independently of their respective nations' specific realities and needs: global rules to a global planet. As unrealistic as this seems to be, this is the story we are told. And we believe it because technology has already taken us half way there.

How could we even think about globalization when we know that religion is still a main issue among peoples. While polytheism has ruled the world for centuries, monotheism rules most countries in the world today. This might explain why religion is a source of discrimination, disagreement, disunion, and massacres. People born and raised in the same country kill each other because they don't share the same religious beliefs. Fighting is not enough; opponents should be exterminated in views of creating a "pure" race or a "pure" culture. Not believing in the same God or not believing in God at all has become a reason for discrimination. This is contemporary barbarism.

Levi-Strauss (1979) had already stated that differences are not harmful and should not be overcome. "It is only through difference that progress has been made" (p. 20). Globalization and overcommunication tend to create the feeling that what happens in one part of the world should happen in other parts of the world as if context meant nothing. In order for a culture to be really itself and to produce something, they should be convinced of their originality. In other words, unification cramps creativity and hinders multiculturalism.

Globalization Brings Us Together and Sets Us Apart

When a brand attempts to reconfigure its image to be everything to all cultures, it gives up its uniqueness in an effort to be ultra-accessible. In doing so, they tend to lose the cultural identity having defined them. A brand is more than a name. A successful brand is an icon, a powerful expression of a cultural archetype. Being loyal to their culture helps the brands to transcend time. When the brand's nationality is well known, it helps with the attraction, admiration, and loyalty, as long as the cultural stereotypes are positive. Examples of companies using their nationality as an added value are Rolex, Versace, and Armani.

Rolex sports a flag from Switzerland on their flagship storefronts around the world as does Versace with the Italian flag. More recently, Valentino launched an advertising campaign with the tagline "Born in Rome." These multinational companies might standardize and globalize most of their products and advertising campaigns, which is easier to be done for luxury brands, without losing their cultural identity. On the other hand, the French company L'Oréal uses an adapted marketing strategy to each country, which can be well explained by the nature of their products. As a matter of fact, peoples' hair and skin are different depending not only on the race but also on the country's climate and culture. Thus, their skin and body care products as well as their makeup and shampoos are locally adapted. In some cases, new products are created to specific markets, such as whitening skin care for Asian countries while similar products for a tan glow are sold in Europe and in the United States. The standards of beauty are not universal. In addition to these multinational adaptations, the company knows that there are different races in each country, so their lines of products should be very broad to suit each type of skin and hair within the same country. Their communication strategy often featuring local celebrities reflects the brand's multicultural marketing strategy.

Many people resist globalization because they feel that globalization tears their roots out from under them. Being part of the world community will make them less themselves. Culture shows us who we are.

We can't expect that there will be only one culture and one civilization in the world. This won't happen because there will always be contradictions: homogenization on the one hand and distinctions on the other hand. The more a civilization becomes homogenized, the more internal lines of separation become apparent, because unification generates frustration of not being able to be oneself. It removes all authenticity from the picture. To understand cultures, we need to study their underlying structure. We look like we are all the same wearing the same brands everywhere, attending the same events, fighting the same "bad guys," and communicating through the same channels. In other words, we are exposed to the same globalized stories, but because our cultures are structured differently, our differences became apparent through our personal practices, which lead to acceptance or rejection from others.

With the globalization of companies has come the globalization of stories. And with technology those stories travel in real time. Movies, TV shows, social media, and video games tell borderless stories so that beliefs can be homogenized. And as stories are never neutral, it is expected that everyone, independently of their culture, race, or gender, believe in them and behave accordingly. We should all agree about who the bad guys are and who the good guys are, which is easy when the story we are told shows only one version of reality and, consequently, everyone is expected to comply with it, otherwise they are rejected. We should all agree to the options offered to us as being the best ones without going any further into exploring other options, and as we are trained to immediacy, we don't waste our time to fact-check or to analyze, we just go with the flow.

This is an invitation to cramping our creativity, to losing our personalities, and to depriving us from our own opinions and visions of life. It is the best way of turning a fascinating multicultural world into a boring one-size-fits-all culture. Fortunately, we know that this will never happen, because unlike global cultures, which are memory-less, real cultures are deep rooted in their historical heritage. Globalization stories might work to persuade peoples from all cultures to buy the same brands and share similar habits, but they can't replace folklore, myths, and beliefs having been built to last. Cultural roots are well planted and cannot be easily unrooted.

Multiculturalism and tolerance imply acceptance of others as they are, rather than changing others to be like us. Trying to make everyone look and think the same way is imperialism. What is the point in telling terrible stories about past colonialism if we accept to be colonized by an imperialistic globalization today? During the colonial era, there was more ignorance and colonizers only knew their own culture which they would impose on less-evolved civilizations as per their own judgment. But their judgment was wrong, because in several of these countries, native populations were more evolved than their colonizers. Because today we are supposed to be smart and evolved, imperialism shouldn't be accepted and yet people seem to be not only happy but also proud to be part of an impersonal mob. Rather than think, people follow. Rather than decide, they are influenced. Rather than create, they share and reshare.

As humans, we are supposed to be more evolved than robots, yet, we do what our devices tell us to do. When your phone doesn't support new apps, you need to buy a brand new one. When your computer slows down, you should buy the most recent one: lighter, faster, with a beautiful design and long lasting battery. Few months later, you will start the same process all over again.

In the old times, people will blindly follow what was decided by their tribes, without questioning any decisions. Also, not all people in the tribes had the same level of knowledge and power. Despite the fact that we are today in the so-called "information era" and that information is accessible to everybody, virtual communities behave just like the old tribes. Communities, other than cultural communities, are taking over multiculturalism. For example, the way flags are currently used is a clear proof of it. Originally, flags would represent a nation, that is, a culture. The colors and the symbols displayed on flags tell part of the countries' history, that is why flags belong to and represent the countries' cultures. Flags are storytellers.

Due to the emergence of the nationalist movement in the latter part of the 18th century—in which nations around the world developed an earnest desire to represent their country and people on an international stage—the civilian use of national flags became popular. To every country on the planet, the national flag is an inextricable part of their culture. Therefore, a flag is meant to identify a location: when you land in a foreign country or when you cross borders on a road, a different flag indicates that you are entering a different country. Do you remember that flag planted on the Moon in 1969? National flags are displayed in all government and public buildings in their own countries and before embassies and consulates abroad, meaning that when you are inside these buildings you should behave by their laws and regulations: you are in a foreign territory.

Flags representing nations are bound to strict rules when handling them—the flag code: never touch the ground and be folded in a very specific way, among others. That is why the utmost disrespect done against a flag and by extension, against the country it represents, is turning the back to it or burning it. It is a clear message of rejection of that country and of its culture. Disrespecting a flag symbolizes a narrative of humiliation and sometimes of revenge against the targeted country. It is an illegal way of showing disagreement with its government, population, and culture.

National flags feature colors and symbols that tell the story of their nation. The stars on the U.S. flag represent the 50 states (colonies) coming together to create a united country, but the stars on the Australian flag represent the Southern Cross, symbol of the southern hemisphere along with the country's cultural heritage and present belonging to the British Commonwealth represented by the British flag. Few years ago, there was a debate in New Zealand about updating their national flag, and those opposed to such a change argued that the new flag would not legitimate their past history. Today, flags are used to represent communities which are the opposite of nations. Nations have a long-lasting shared culture; communities have shared interests which can be short termed depending on the evolution of those interests based on current events. Communities' flags represent an ambition, an objective; it is not at all the same story. But the use of a flag by a community gives the illusion of a nation and this is why people tend to call them culture.

The use of flags by communities reinforces the confusion between what culture is and what a community stands for.

Implications for Multicultural Marketing

As long as people will be kept confused between race and culture, community and culture, they will be unable to understand other cultures. There can be two main consequences to this. First, people might believe in globalization and never care about figuring out other cultures by assuming that we are all the same. Second, and more frustrating, they might be less open to diversity and reject everyone who doesn't belong to their community, whether it is a cultural community or not. These are not good news to multiculturalism and to multicultural marketing. Thus, companies should understand that adapting their marketing strategies to each country, while assuming that all the people in that country are the same, can lead to disappointing outcomes. Companies should mix their multinational and multicultural marketing strategies in order to be successful and thoroughly satisfy their multicultural clients.

Key Takeaways From Chapter 7

- Of all people, marketers are the ones who should not get confused with concepts relating to diversity, culture, race, and community.
- Marketers should include a measure of openness to diversity in their market research to estimate potential acceptance of foreign brands.
- Universalism is more of a goal than of reality; cultures are specific.

CHAPTER 8

Decoding Multicultural Marketing

What's the Story?

Once upon a time, people believed in myths, and one of them was globalization. Because of this belief, companies would not care about cultural differences among and within countries and would try to sell the same products to everyone. This lack of cultural awareness led several companies to big financial losses and spoiled their brand reputation abroad. Another myth was that multinational and multicultural marketing were the same. It was time to help marketers to understand that cultural codes are critical and know how to decode them when they are facing dilemmas.

Marketing is the quest for customer loyalty. By satisfying customers' specific needs, companies try to acquire and retain a consumer base for as long as possible. The role of marketing is to produce the right product, sell it at the right price, give customers access to it, and promote it to inform and persuade the targeted consumer market.

Among the multiple factors that affect consumers' decisions in the choice of products and loyalty to brands is their cultural background. The illusion of a global world has led multiple companies to fail when they deploy their activities abroad. Companies that assume that all consumers around the world are the same can't be expected to understand or even consider the fact that consumers with different cultural backgrounds living in the same country and in the same city have different needs and expectations from companies too. It is all about cultural differences. While after several failures companies start taking cultural differences into account when they venture abroad, they still ignore multiculturalism within their domestic markets. This explains why multicultural marketing is either not used or misunderstood.

Multicultural marketing can be defined as marketing efforts addressing culturally different target markets. Unlike international marketing, which addresses culturally different target markets in different countries, multicultural marketing targets consumers with different cultural backgrounds within the same country.

Thus, in the same city, marketers might want to address each cultural community with an adapted offer. As an illustration, I conducted a project with my multicultural marketing course students in the city of Chicago in 2022, the city being home to more than 20 different cultures. In teams, students had free choice of a cultural community to work on. They picked three of them: Chinese, Japanese, and Mexican. They proceeded with a cultural analysis of their chosen cultural communities, studied the three different target consumers, and designed their respective marketing strategies for launching a new product in the food industry. The cultural differences among the three cultures studied by them appeared to be of utmost importance for the targeted consumers to accept the new products. The main differences rested on the amount of spices, serving sizes relating to family sizes, types of sauces, and the ability of adding customers' personal touch to the food among other cultural specificities. The need for bilingual packaging was also a difference to be noted, as well as the products' names. The founder of the company and their marketing team were absolutely amazed because they would have never even thought of exploring cultural differences within the same city, but experts in multicultural marketing are expected to know that cultural differences persist even if people live in the same city.

Because there is such confusion between race and culture and between multicultural and international, companies end up neglecting cultural differences and addressing all markets the same way, which causes frustrations among the consumers and subsequent financial losses to the companies. By believing that all consumers aim for the same benefits from products, companies are unable to tell enticing stories that each cultural community within the same city can relate to. This is how they miss part of their domestic markets. Ironically, and as much as companies can be somehow excused for failing abroad for lack of cultural knowledge, they are supposed to know very well their domestic markets.

The study described earlier very clearly uncovered the need for adaptation of the marketing strategy to each of the cultures that were studied in the project. Adaptations were needed in terms of the taste of the product, the serving sizes, the brand name, the packaging, the price point, the distribution channels, and the promotional activities. Briefly said, each cultural community required a specific marketing strategy to be addressed to them.

Awareness Precedes Clarity and Clarity Precedes Results

The lack of cultural awareness leads companies to assume that all people are the same everywhere and that they would happily accept a standardized offer. Nothing could be further from the truth. Consumers are culturally sensitive and expect companies to be respectful of their cultural specificities.

According to Storti (1999), there are several stages of cultural awareness:

- *Unconscious incompetence (blissful ignorance)*
  People are not aware that there are cultural differences between people; hence, it does not occur to them that they may be making cultural mistakes or that they may be misinterpreting much of the behavior going on around them. They have no reason at this stage not to trust their intuition.
- *Conscious incompetence (troubling ignorance)*
  People realize that there are differences between the way they and people from other cultures behave, though they understand very little about just what these differences are, how numerous they might be, or how deep they might go. They know there is a problem but can't measure its size. They are less sure of their intuition and realize that there are things they don't understand. They wonder whether they will be able to figure foreigners out.
- *Conscious competence (deliberate sensitivity)*
  People know that there are cultural differences between people; they know what these differences are; and they try to modify their

own behavior to be sensitive to these differences. But all this doesn't come naturally yet and requires considerable effort to behave in culturally sensate ways. But they are much more aware of how their behavior is being interpreted by other people. It is the beginning of the process of replacing old intuitions with new ones. It becomes easier to figure out the foreigners by becoming objective.

- *Unconscious competence (spontaneous sensitivity)*
  People no longer have to think about what they are doing in order to be culturally sensitive. Culturally appropriate behavior becomes natural, and intuition can be trusted because it has been reconditioned by what people know about cross-cultural interactions.

Understanding the cultural awareness process is crucial to companies and consumers alike. If we are not aware, we don't know what to expect from others or from ourselves. And because there is no clarity without awareness, marketers should be well aware of cultural differences within the same country and the same city to clearly set cultural communities apart before making strategic decisions if they want to have a long-lasting relationship with their customers.

As a matter of fact, multicultural marketers should never wonder if there are cultural differences within a given population. Rather, they should know that they exist, study these differences, and give a multicultural perspective to their marketing strategies in regards to the different cultural populations.

You Never Get a Second Chance to Have a First Experience

With the words above, Rapaille (2007, 21) describes the crucial role of imprints in our perception of life, in our behavior, and in our choices in life. The author has conducted extensive work in decoding cultures. He defines culture code as the unconscious meaning we apply to any given thing or object via the culture in which we are raised. We know that cultures are different from one another, but we need to understand that these differences lead to processing the same information in different ways.

We already explained the role of emotions in the learning process as well as the importance of experience in creating memorable relationships between consumers and brands. We now know that there is a clear connection between learning and emotions. It is impossible to learn without emotions. The stronger the emotions are, the more clearly an experience is apprehended. "The combination of the experience and its accompanying emotions creates something known widely as an imprint" (Lorenz: in Rapaille 2007, 6). Once an imprint occurs, it strongly conditions our thought processes and shapes our future actions. Each imprint makes us more of who we are. The combination of imprints defines us.

The culture code is the unconscious meaning we apply to any given thing or object via the culture in which we are raised; thus, cultural codes reveal the deep understanding and feelings people have about their surroundings. Because they are unconscious, they are often overlooked by companies. Yet, the way to understanding humans and thus consumer behavior in multicultural settings is by adding the cultural unconscious to the Freudian theory in which the unconscious guides each person's behavior in unique ways and to the Jungian collective unconscious that guides each of us as members of the human species (Rapaille 2007).

The codes themselves do not pass judgment on a particular culture. When cultures change, the changes occur in the same way as in our brains via powerful imprints. These imprints alter the "reference system" of the culture, and the significance is passed down to subsequent generations. We all behave, or are supposed to behave, in accordance with a set of rules established by others: legal and educational institutions, family, friends, and any other groups we belong to. When these rules change because of external influence, the behaviors change too because now there is a different reference system. These changes come with new generations and the contact with other cultures.

When a company knows that associating a product with a certain code will trigger negative feelings, it can choose to sidestep that code completely. Better yet, companies that uncover the culture codes are more likely to design marketing strategies in accordance with each different culture, because their codes are different. In other words, figuring out the cultural codes enables companies to tell their consumers stories that make sense to them.

Rapaille (2007) came up with five principles for uncovering cultural codes:

- *Principle 1: You can't believe what people say.*
  When asked direct questions, respondents tend to give the answers they believe the questioner wants to hear. Their responses come from their cortexes, the part of their brains that controls intelligence rather than emotions or instincts. They ponder and process a question, and the answer is the product of their deliberation. We should always find a reason to explain our behavior, even if that reason is "because everybody else is doing so." While shopping is joyful and life-affirming, buying sends a very different unconscious message. Buying signals the end of shopping. Thus, retailers need to consider this buying/shopping tension. Alibis give rational reasons for doing the things they do. They are legitimate. They give us good reasons to consume. It is in our reptilian brains that the real answers lie. This is where our instincts are housed. It is during the state between sleep and wakefulness that we have better access to our memories and instincts.

  This leads us to the behavioral contradictions we can observe in people. They say what is socially accepted but act differently when following their instincts. In other words, there is a gap between the stories we tell and our reality. One example of such a contradiction is all those who show themselves fighting slavery while purchasing clothes and devices manufactured by people who are not called slaves, today, but don't live and work in better conditions than the 17th-century slaves.

- *Principle 2: Emotion is the energy required to learn anything.*
  Emotions create a series of mental connections that are reinforced by repetition. That is why we do most of our learning when we are children. Our mental structure is constructed by the age of seven. We can remember where we were, with whom, and even what we were wearing during experiences that have marked our existence.

  There is a difference between teaching and learning. You only learn if you want to learn, independent of having a teacher lecture you. If, during the lecture, your attention is turned to the messages on your phone or to any other sources of distraction, you won't learn anything. Learning requires engagement on both sides; otherwise, we wouldn't learn anything from books!

- *Principle 3: The structure, not the content is the message.*
  The important part is the connections between the different elements of the story. The key to understanding the real meaning behind our actions is to understand their structure. The structures are at three levels: biological structure—DNA; cultural structure—the way elements of culture are organized creates the unique identity of each culture; and individual structure—our experience.

  That is why a story without context doesn't make any sense. Anything without a structure seems to be too loose to enable sense-making. We always need to know who, when, where, and how; place all these in context; and establish relationships among them to understand the story.

- *Principle 4: There is a window in time for imprinting and the meaning of the imprint varies from one culture to another.*
  Most of us imprint the meanings of the things most central to our lives by the age of seven, when the emotional state of the child changes in a single hour. After this phase, children are driven by logic. Most people are exposed to only one culture before the age of seven, as they spend most of this time at home and within the local environment.

  This is why the extremely strong imprints placed in their subconscious at this early age are determined by the culture in which they are raised. And this is also why people from different cultures have such different reactions to the same things. In addition, it shows us that cultural differences should not be ignored. The culture you were raised in remains part of your life and defines your values for the rest of your life, even if you move to other countries and interact with people from other cultures.

- *Principle 5: To access the meaning of an imprint within a particular culture, you must learn the code for that imprint.*
  Even our most arbitrary actions are the result of the trips we take down to our mental connections. We take these trips hundreds of times a day, making decisions about what to wear, what to eat,

and where to go. There is a code required to make these journeys. Our brains supply these codes subconsciously. Codes affect our responses to everything, and they are not universal.

Your behavior, the brands you use, the places you go, and the people you are related to carry your culture and tell stories about you.

As cultures are different, laws and experiences are different too. Driving a car for the first time when you are 16 years old is not the same experience as driving it when you are 18. The same applies to the consumption of alcohol when you are 18 or 21 years old. These legal considerations are specific to different countries, which prompts the question of the legal age for reaching adulthood. If you get your driver's license when you are 16, vote when you are 18, and can consume alcohol when you are 21, at what age do you become an adult? Is this a gradual way of reaching adulthood? On the other hand, in other countries, you become an adult when you turn 18 because you can get your driver's license, vote, and drink alcohol all at once. In other words, you become an adult overnight. Because of that, two persons from these two different legal contexts will have different imprints of their entrance in the adult world.

The Multicultural Marketers' Dilemmas

Marketers' jobs have never been this sensitive. Practicing marketing turned into a double-edged sword. Whatever companies do can generate either adhesion or a backlash. If they don't speak about diversity, backlash. If they do, backlash.

This prompts the question of how much political involvement companies should have and make public knowing that it can be very detrimental to their products and brand. In 1997, Disney launched the movie *Kundun*, an American epic biographical film based on the life and writings of Tenzin Gyatso, the 14th Dalai Lama, the exiled political and spiritual leader of Tibet, and displaying Chinese oppression of the Tibetan people. The backlash was immediate, and the negotiations about the opening of Disneyland in Shanghai were frozen. The park was finally opened in 2016, after Disney apologized for the film and agreed to keep only 43 percent of the shares of the park. Other than the financial losses engendered by the delay, the backlash on the brand reputation is hardly forgettable.

Among the biggest challenges for marketers today are branding and advertising. In other words, the biggest challenge is to tell the right story to the right people in the right way. The risk goes far beyond people rejecting the companies' products like they used to do before; now people can reject and cancel the company altogether.

Companies are often criticized for portraying only one type of consumer in their communications. Consumers' associations, among others, claim, on behalf of diversity and inclusion, that all types of people should always be portrayed in all advertisements. We know that it is not possible from a practical standpoint, because of the number of cultures existing in a given country, but more importantly, it is not true to the marketing concept. The rule of thumb for a successful marketing strategy is segmenting the market based on several relevant criteria, clearly setting different consumers apart, and selecting the target(s) market(s) to address with the chosen marketing strategy. Marketers then decide on the positioning of their brand when addressing their target(s) market(s) by telling them an enticing story about the benefits of their products and the unique solutions they can bring to these unique consumers' problems. Thus, the obligation of portraying everyone is the opposite of what marketers should do: address a specific target market. How to address the chosen target market without being charged for discrimination today?

Positioning a brand has always been a challenge for marketers. It should be clear enough for the targeted consumers to understand it; it should be credible enough to entice the consumers; and it should be different enough to distinguish it from its competitors. Often, there is a discrepancy between the positioning (story) the company wants to convey and the story heard by consumers. This happens when the brand positioning is blurred and consumers can't understand it; that is, they can't set that brand apart from its competitors, because the specific benefits that it can provide them are not made clear. Also, they might not relate to the brand or to the people portrayed in the communication.

In diverse markets, consumers might go against the brand because they are unable to identify with their products, their positioning, and the way consumers are portrayed in their communication. Always aiming at serving their own communities, consumers protest if the brand doesn't address them directly, even if they don't belong to the targeted market. By trying to please everyone, some brands are losing their clear positioning in a diffuse, competitive market. It is a real dilemma for multicultural marketers, because one of the main advantages of segmentation and targeting is to reduce the number of competitors in each market segment. Thus, if their brands should please everyone, the segmentation loses its utility, and the competition is as fierce as if companies addressed the entirety of the market rather than specific segments of it. Another implication of this decision is that by trying to please everyone, the company can end up pleasing no one.

Because positioning is conveyed through communication, other than portraying the "right" consumers, advertising should tell a story that resonates with the consumers it targets. This is more complex in a multicultural environment because of the idiosyncrasies of each culture. Thus, the use of humor or accepted behaviors should be well thought out because they differ across cultural values. For example, the use of comedy in advertising is a real field in marketing. Humor attracts people and makes them feel good. But humor has no universal definition, and what can seem funny in some cultures might not be perceived the same way in others. In addition, when the comedy involves celebrities, marketers should make sure that those celebrities are well known and positively perceived by all multicultural consumers.

Targeting is choosing the people who can be potentially interested in the stories the companies tell. Once the target market is chosen, companies promote their brands through communication strategies. The brand name is supposed to tell a sense-making story to the targeted consumers. But how to choose the name of a product without being accused of discrimination? Should we change brand names that have been around for a century or so? How do we deal with the customer loyalty to our brand built over time if we change it now? How should we depict people in advertising? If we acknowledge ethnic differences, we are racist; if we don't, we are racist. Should we portray same-sex couples, the same or different colors of skin, and all genders, knowing that none of these have anything to do with culture? The alternatives are overwhelming, as are the risks linked to all these decisions. How to know what is the "right thing to do"? How to address specific target markets without being accused of discrimination?

When Uncle Ben's produced by Mars Inc. and Aunt Jemima brand names were created, they would portray the caring and generous family members feeding their families. The words uncle and aunt imply closeness and personal and emotional relationships other than blood ties. Today, it is considered racist and demeaning because both Uncle and Aunt would supposedly be serving families other than their own. The brand names were changed and lost their personality: Ben's Original doesn't mean much. There can't be any emotion enticing consumers to buy such a brand name. The same applies to Aunt Jemima, which now carries the impersonal name of Pearl Milling Company. This brand will never be a myth. Surprisingly, nothing was said about Sun-Maid raisins brand, which has the word "maid," in it and could be perceived as being even more demeaning than uncle or aunt, and the picture of the maid on the packaging. Where does the difference rest, one might wonder?

The main question here is how to secure brand longevity if marketers need to rethink their brand names every time a new story is told to influence people's beliefs? How to keep up with the changes in reference systems? If the changes are gradual, companies can gradually adjust their marketing strategies, because marketers are part of the same changing context. But when the changes are sudden, triggered by one event, marketers can't know if that will be a long-lasting trend or just an ephemeral claim.

Although following social changes with new or updated products is not that much of an issue, brand name decisions are so. Brands are meant to be stable and permanent. Being unable to measure the longevity of the trend, marketers take big risks in changing or not changing their brand names. Products come and go, but brands are meant to stay. Consumers have a functional relationship with products but an emotional relationship with brands. They are loyal to brands, not to products. A brand name change introduces instability in this hedonic relationship. It is a real dilemma for marketers.

Products go through several adaptations to better suit cultural differences. Biological differences explain product adaptation. Differences in the hair, the skin, the shape of the body, and the taste explain product adaptation, but the brands remain the same. People from different cultures purchase products adapted to their specific needs under the same brand names used in different cultures for people with different physical traits. Cultural differences do explain product creation and adaptation. In the food industry, for instance, depending on the culture, the food should be spicy, fish- or meat-based, vegetarian, vegan, Halal, Kosher, and so on. But the brand names can remain the same. These product adaptations are imperative to comply with some cultures while optional in others.

A brand name is coupled with a logo that has a specific color as its identity. Often, the tone of color they use is patented along with the name and the logo. But colors have cultural meanings too. Color is fundamental to our experience of the world around us. Colors are light being reflected off the surface of objects and back to our eyes. Different things are different colors because they absorb some wavelengths of the visible light spectrum, while others bounce off. So, in a way, the color we perceive an object to be is precisely the color it isn't!

Colors are named after cultures too—Indian yellow, Naples yellow, Dutch orange, Prussian blue, Egyptian blue, each one having a story behind it. Colors also have paradoxical meanings: black is dark and evil (witches, black cats) but also glamorous, sophisticated, and elegant, like a black dress (La Petite Robe Noire, a perfume from Guerlain). Red is passion (Campari), sensuality but also violence, blood, and signs of interdiction (stop, do not enter, red light).

Designing a Multicultural Marketing Strategy

There are several steps in designing a multicultural marketing strategy, and they are all of equal importance. The first step is understanding that cultural roots explain several behaviors and choices made by consumers by integrating what we know about cultures as studied by relevant researchers. To do so, you should get acquainted with the main cultural orientations.

The second step is to perform a cultural analysis of the cultures to be targeted with your multicultural marketing strategy. Use the cultural analysis grid to do so. The third step is to incorporate your understanding of culture into your marketing strategy. The fourth and last step is establishing your multicultural marketing plan to operationalize your well-designed strategy. Let's study each one of these steps, one by one.

Main Cultural Orientations

Geert Hofstede (1984) created a 6D model to analyze cultural dimensions: power distance, individualism, masculinity, uncertainty avoidance, long-term orientation, and indulgence. He assigned scores to different cultures on a 1 to 100 scale for these variables. Later, Hofstede and Hofstede (2005) stated that the world is full of confrontations between people, groups, and nations that think, feel, and act differently. At the same time, these people are exposed to common problems that demand cooperation for their solution.

The authors see culture as mental programming, because all people carry within themselves patterns of thinking, feeling, and potentially acting that they have learned throughout their lifetimes. Much of this information was acquired in early childhood, because that is when a person is most susceptible to learning and assimilating. As soon as certain patterns have established themselves within people's minds, they must unlearn them before being able to learn something different—and unlearning is more difficult than learning for the first time.

The authors also point out that culture should be distinguished from human nature and personality. Human nature is what all people have in common. Culture is always a collective phenomenon, because it is at least partly shared with those who live in or have lived within the same social environment. Culture is learned, not innate. It comes from one's social environment, not from one's genes. Personality is one's unique set of mental programs that need not be shared with any other human beings. It is based on traits that are partly inherited from the individual's unique set of genes and partly learned.

Trompenaars and Hampden-Turner (2006) explain cultural differences as each culture choosing specific solutions to certain problems that reveal themselves as dilemmas. They stated that working in international settings is about reconciling the dilemmas, as shown in Table 8.1.

Table 8.1 Reconciling dilemmas in Trompenaars and Hampden-Turner's cultural dimensions

Affectivity	Affective neutrality
Feeling, emotion, and gratification	Practical or moral considerations
Self-orientation	**Communitarianism**
Self-interest	Group goals and interests
Universalism	**Particularism**
Using common standards to evaluate situations and groups	Using different standards to evaluate situations and groups
Ascription	**Achievement**
Stressing who you are	Stressing what you do or have done
Specificity	**Diffuseness**
Interaction for specific purposes	Interaction across a wide range of activities

Edward Hall (1976) identified two extremes of a cultural dimension, depending on the cultural context. After having analyzed 11 cultures, he placed them on a continuum, stretching from high-context to low-context cultures. He defined "low-context cultures" as the ones in which the communication is more objective: with a small portion of nonverbal messages and less dependent on relationship building. In these cultures, social and professional lives are clearly separated. On the other end of the continuum, he placed "high-context cultures," which are more implicit. They add a considerable amount of nonverbal communication and incorporate personal relationships and ritual celebrations into their professional practices.

In other words, low-context cultural environments expect and reinforce making meaning explicit. They block out the potential interference of nonverbal or other contextual sources. In high-context cultures, the successful exchange of information hinges on the ability to apply a shared and implicit framework of interpretation to a message.

Hall also explained differences in time management by defining some cultures as being polychronic and others as being monochronic.

Polychronic individuals go back and forth on the same activity, pausing when they are interrupted by other tasks or other people. They don't mind stopping something in favor of something else and then coming back to what they were doing before. Also, they feel comfortable when someone cuts them off during conversations and do not get lost when many people speak simultaneously. Monochronic people schedule and allocate specific time slots for each activity. They lose their place when they are interrupted and get very disturbed when several people talk at once. Moreover, in monochronic cultures, meetings start and finish on time. The agenda is followed from top to bottom, and once a topic is already discussed, it is not revisited.

These differences in time management are meaningful. Assign a monochronic and a polychronic person the same three tasks. After a while, the polychronic will be able to tell you a bit about each one and how she is handling them, but she will probably be late to hand them in and might negotiate the deadline. At the same time, the monochronic will only be able to tell you about the first task, because she will not have started any others before she is done with that one. She will be able to go deeper into the description of what she has been doing for the first task but will be unable to tell you about the remaining ones. This might be misleading, as you might think that the monochronic has not understood that there are three tasks to be done. However, she will respect the deadline and finish the three projects on time.

Richard Lewis (2006, 2012) states that human beings organize their lives around two core features: values and communication. These elements usually remain constant in a person's behavioral makeup. This is principally true because people—when faced with the trials and vicissitudes of life—have a strong urge to seek security in traditional behavioral refugees.

Lewis' LMR model divides cultures into three categories:

1. *Linear-active people* tend to be task-oriented, highly organized planners who complete action chains by doing one thing at a time, preferably in accordance with a linear agenda. Speech is for information and depends largely on facts and figures.

2. *Multiactive people* are loquacious, emotional, and impulsive. They attach great importance to family, meetings, relationships, compassion, and human warmth. They like to do many things at the same time and are poor followers of agendas. Speech is for opinions.

3. *Reactive people* are good listeners and rarely initiate action or discussion. They prefer to first hear and establish the other's position, then react to it and formulate their own opinion. Reactives listen before they leap. Speech is for creating harmony.

Schwartz and Bisky (1987) studied the motivational goals underlying cultural values and identified 10 fundamental values. Schwartz's works represent the most comprehensive exploration of cultural values to date. Their typology, presented here, has been found to be universal and stable across gender, age, socioeconomic groups, cultures, and generations.

- Achievement (personal success through demonstrating competence according to social standards)
- Hedonism (pleasure and sensuous gratification)
- Stimulation (excitement, novelty, and challenge in life)
- Self-direction (independent thought and action; choosing, creating, and exploring)
- Universalism (understanding, appreciation, tolerance, caring about humanity, and nature)
- Benevolence (preserving and enhancing the welfare of loved ones, friends, and family)
- Conformity (restraint of actions and inclinations)
- Tradition (respect, commitment, and acceptance of the customs and ideas that traditional culture or religion provide the self)
- Security (safety and harmony, and the stability of society, relationships, and self)
- Power (social status and prestige, control, or dominance over people and resources)

The authors also empirically demonstrated that, if you place these values in a mathematical two-dimensional space, they will form the so-called circumplex structure: the values with similar motivational goals will end up closer to each other, and the values with conflicting motivational goals will be further apart.

Walker and colleagues (2003) define culture as a complex phenomenon that can be determined by three axioms:

- *Axiom 1*: Cultural boundaries are not national boundaries. Although it is easier to describe nations as cultures and generalize behaviors, there are cultural commonalities across countries, and there are subcultures in each country.

- *Axiom 2*: Culture is a shared pattern of ideas, emotions, and behaviors. Cultures operate on both a conscious and an unconscious level, and their characteristics are carried by both groups and individuals.
- *Axiom 3*: Cultures reflect distinctive value orientations at various levels. The specificity of culture lies in the difference between "in" and "out" groups. People who share the same culture sense that they are different from people who do not belong to that culture.

Finally, House and Colleagues (2004) created the 10 cultural orientations model, which presents a framework for exploring and mapping components of culture at any level. It is the cornerstone of the cultural orientation approach and provides a common language and comprehensive lens for analyzing cultural phenomena and cross-cultural encounters. This set of cultural dimensions summarizes the main aspects that can explain cultural differences and cause misunderstandings in business settings. They are described in Table 8.2.

Once you acquire an overall understanding of the multiple facets of cultures, you can proceed with the second step in designing your multicultural marketing strategy and perform a cultural analysis of the cultures

Table 8.2 The 10 cultural orientations

Cultural Orientations	Characteristics
Environment	Control/harmony/constraint
Time	Monochronic/polychronic, fixed/fluid, past/present/future
Action	Being/doing
Communication	High/low context, direct/indirect, formal/informal
Space	Private/public
Power	Hierarchy/equality
Individualism	Individualism/collectivism, universalism/particularism
Competitiveness	Competitive/cooperative
Structure	Order/flexibility
Thinking	Deductive/inductive, Linear/systemic

you will address with your marketing strategy. Use the cultural analysis grid (Table 8.3) to do so. Use one separate grid for each culture.

Cultural Analysis

Table 8.3 Cultural analysis grid

CULTURAL ANALYSIS GRID COUNTRY:	
Relevant history	a) Key dates b) Key events
Geography	Location
	Climate
	Topography

Social institutions	Family
	   a) Nuclear family
	   b) Extended family
	   c) Dynamics of the family
	   d) Female/male roles

	Education
	   a) Primary education
	   b) Secondary education
	   c) Higher education
	   d) Literacy rate

	Political system
	   a) Political structure
	   b) Political parties
	   c) Stability of government
	   d) Special taxes
	   e) Role of local government

	Legal system
	   a) Judiciary system
	   b) Patents, trademarks,…

	Social organizations
	   a) Groups
	   b) Social classes
	   c) Clubs and associations
	   d) Race, ethnicity, subcultures

	Business customs and practices

CULTURAL ANALYSIS GRID COUNTRY:	
Religion	a) Doctrines and structures b) Relationship with people c) Prominent religions d) Powerful and influential cults
Esthetics	a) Visual arts b) Music c) Drama, ballet, opera d) Folklore and relevant symbols
Living conditions	Diet and nutrition a) Meat and vegetable consumption rates b) Typical meals c) Malnutrition rates d) Foods available
	Housing a) Types of housing b) Ownership and rental c) One family or several
	Clothing a) National dress b) Work dress code
	Recreation, sports, and leisure a) Types available b) Percentage of income spent
	Social security and health care
Language	a) Official language(s) b) Spoken and written languages c) Dialects

Marketing Strategy

The third step in designing your multicultural marketing strategy is defining your goals and your strategic terms. You start working on cultural identity. This is each consumer's identification with a specific culture that takes material form in markets. The market provides an interpretative lens for understanding preferences, social constructs, and cultural and sociological forces, which are then reinforced by representations. Such representations are conveyed through stories told by advertising, brand names, logos, and colors.

Now that you acquired a good grasp on cultures and their specific characteristics, you are able to answer the following questions:

- Do the chosen ethnic communities have different wants and needs?
- Are special marketing strategies required to effectively target them?
- What kind of thinking is needed?
- What traditional marketing strategies can still be used?
- What are the main pitfalls to avoid?

Some wants and needs can be similar across some of the cultural communities, which can lead to some standardization of certain variables of the marketing strategy. But some others might highly differ and require adaptation.

It is imperative to understand that, when dealing with multicultural marketing, marketers should:

1. Avoid monolithic thinking—people are different.
2. Speak their consumers' language—decode cultural codes.
3. Go beyond *one size fits all*—universal needs.
4. Understand ethnic diversity—avoid basic assumptions.
5. Understand potential and future consumers—age/sex/gender/ culture and so on.
6. Tell each cultural community stories that resonate with them.

Stating that all customers are different is an understatement. The secret of success resides in identifying such differences and being able to comply with all of them. To do so, multicultural marketers should understand the typology of cultural consumers:

- *Cultural experimentalism* consists of continuously seeking exposure to products and experiences from other cultures.
- *Cultural extensionism* is a slow and cautious strategy where people progress step by step beyond their comfort zone to adopt the products of other cultures.

- *Cultural purism* describes a reasoned and selective approach toward culturally cued products, which restricts consumption to specific cultures.
- *Cultural passivity* describes a form of inertia and a lack of engagement with other cultures.

In addition to segmenting customers based on their ethnic backgrounds, multicultural marketers should also identify those who correspond to each of the previous types of consumers and know how to address them differently. As a matter of fact, consumers from cultural experimentalism and cultural passivity, for instance, are opposed to each other and can't be persuaded with the same arguments. Different stories are needed to entice different types of consumers.

Multicultural Marketing Mix

When it comes to the 4Ps of the marketing mix, multicultural marketers should observe the following factors:

Product-related factors: Different patterns of consumption within and among ethnic groups, explanations for variations including cultural and generational factors, socioeconomic characteristics, and the symbolic role of products in identity formation within and among ethnic groups.

Price-related factors: Consumers' price sensitivity, consumers' information search behavior, and the cost-effective nature of marketing to different cultural communities.

Place-related factors: Shopping activities differ in the number of shopping companions and types of stores visited, and consumers tend to live around members of their ethnic group.

Promotion-related factors: The appropriateness of different media for various ethnic groups, bilingual language proficiency, multicultural accommodation, and marketing budget spent on ethnic media.

When telling stories to consumers through advertising, multicultural marketers should consider three different models. The so-called *United*

Nations model integrates several ethnic communities, displaying products adapted to each community under the same brand name. It is basically the same product with slight cultural adaptations. The *Cultural Normalization model* has the opposite effect. Rather than acknowledging cultural differences, it integrates consumers from different cultures in the same consumption context with standardized products and brands. Finally, the *Cultural Appropriation model* invites consumers to try products from other cultures.

Storytelling is a marketing tool. A relatable central figure is needed as a protagonist, an individual the target market can relate to or identify with. Often, celebrities praised in specific cultures are called to play this role. Stories can increase emotional connections to the brand, and emotions can influence buying behavior. Marketers should incorporate a desirable objective, goal, motivation, or situation for the consumer to analyze and be enticed by. Because consumer-generated stories allow for active engagement, contributions, and investment in the brand's story, social media is a powerful storytelling tool for marketers as long as they take cultural differences into account.

When it comes to analyzing multicultural consumers' behaviors, marketers can relate to three different types of cultural behaviors. *Cultural imperatives* are specific expectations anchored in cultural customs that the brand should imperatively meet. *Cultural electives* is the option given by consumers to accept something external to their culture. And the *cultural exclusives* are products and brands that consumers from that culture are unwilling to share with consumers from other cultural communities.

The Multicultural Marketing Plan

Once the marketing strategy is designed, the marketing plan will be the guide to putting it into action:

- Define your communities: Cultural segmentation. Identify the cultural communities you can deliver to without generating frustration by standardizing your offer.
- Choose your targets: Select the segment(s) you know better, are stronger than your competitors, and are ready to interact with.

- Establish specific objectives: Be realistic about your objectives in taking into account the size, the income, and the willingness to purchase your products.
- Understand how target consumers relate to your product: Needs, value, usages…. Remember that they are specific to different cultures.
- Position your brand: Be sure to tell a story that resonates with your targets.
- Measure the efficiency of your marketing strategy: Let your consumers tell you their own story about your brand.

Implications for Multicultural Marketing

Although there are significant similarities between multicultural and multinational marketing, it is imperative that marketers understand the differences between both. When dealing with multicultural marketing, marketers should go through the process of understanding and respecting internal cultural differences. In the same way they would study foreign cultures before venturing abroad, marketers should study the cultures involved in the domestic market as part of their segmentation criteria and take cultural differences into account when defining their target markets and positioning their brands.

Key Takeaways From Chapter 8

- One culture equals one coding system. Marketers should be able to decode different cultures.
- A sharp mission statement and unambiguous positioning can help marketers to make appropriate decisions when facing cultural dilemmas.
- Designing a multicultural marketing strategy is a process requiring method and rigor.

Conclusion

Writing and Telling a Successful Multicultural Marketing Story

Multiculturalism is what makes life and marketing fascinating. It is the way out of the boredom of hearing always the same story about the same people, from the same people: routine. It is a new discovery every day. It is a new chapter of the story every single day as if a new character came into the plot to shake up the linear path the story was going through.

Stories are also made of irony. In a globalized world where traveling became accessible and affordable to everyone thanks to new business models such as low-cost airlines, with Airbnb as an option to hotels and Uber for taxis, traveling across countries and getting to know different cultures was supposed to be made easier. Yet, travel plans have been cramped by the pandemic and wars, just like in the old times. It looks like we will be spending more time in our tribes than interacting with others, unless we do it remotely. But thanks to immigration, we live in multicultural countries. We can have a taste of several different cultures without going abroad and this is a benefit that not everyone seems to be able to value. Multicultural marketing should lead the way to interacting with people who live next door but come from different cultures. Marketers should show where and how to enjoy new products, languages, arts, and celebrations.

Successful stories mix adventure with mystery, suspense, humor, romance, and drama. Successful stories are those consumers can relate to. Some brands fail while others succeed with the same type of product. Those who fail didn't tell the right story; those who succeeded did. For instance, the launch of Dasani from Coca Cola Company failed in Europe because the word about the product being purified water rather than mineral water was a story European consumers were unwilling to accept. But American consumers accepted this story, not only because it is an affordable brand for water but also because being purified rather than mineral doesn't resonate with any negative references. But times change and today, even an expensive brand for water named Essentia promising an ionized hydration for being an overarching H_2O is accepted by consumers in the United States, because the market is following the very trendy consumption of energy drinks of all types.

Thus, telling the right story to the right people at the right moment is one of the roles of multicultural marketing. The historical and scientific approaches given in this book aimed at clarifying myths, ideas, and stories told about ourselves. We do share a common story, because we share a common past: we belong to the same species. We are *Homo sapiens*. Yet, we don't belong to the same races and even less to the same cultures. Today we live in diverse countries thanks to colonization and immigration. Ironically, as we celebrate diversity, we fight colonization and immigration.

We know that we are not equal because we don't share the same roots, the same religion, same history, and geography. No one is of "pure blood." Since the time the *sapiens* met the Neanderthals, we have been mixed. Diversity is nothing new. Colonization created new ethnicities and was responsible for the evolution of cultures. Cultures are dynamic because they change when they meet other cultures and immigration is a big accelerator of cultural evolution.

The stories we are told about our past and our present seem to be paradoxical. We preach universalism while we claim diversity. It is impossible. Universalism imposes uniformity, which is technically the opposite of multiculturalism. If you want to enjoy multiculturalism, you should take people as they are: unique. There is nothing universal about humans. We are biologically and culturally different. Only the laws of physics are universal.

But we like stories that make us shiver. If we don't have the bad guys, we can't have this kind of sensation. Thus, we create a paradoxical world to live in. The binary approach to reality opposes good to evil and true to false as if these were the only two options. We live in a constant dilemma opposing right to wrong, what creates considerable tension by the risk of making the wrong decision.

Science teaches us that the world is not all made of dichotomy. Indeed, the core of quantum physics is the acknowledgment of several simultaneous states of an object and of the theory of the many worlds. Thus the ideological approach to the binary reality opposes ideas to facts because an ideology is a structure that thinks for each individual rather than yielding to critical thinking.

Contemporary Stories Are Old Stories

The ideology around the planet turned the concerns about the environment into concerns about pollution before it turned to energy, which is the only focus of all green concerns today. In other words, energy (electric) became the synonym of ecology. But air pollution is just one kind of pollution, which, by the way, won't be solved with the "100 percent electric" policy, and that is only one among other options to replace oil. Because this is the story we are told every day all day, we never think about the other kinds of pollution. All of our senses suffer every day from noise, aggressive visuals, disgusting smells, and poisonous food.

While we criticize air pollution, we buy more and more online. Each time that you are home delivered, you increase the number of transportations and thus of air pollution. If you multiply the number of home deliveries by millions of people buying online around the world, you will be shocked with how much pollution you contribute to create. You don't even think about it, because the story you are told is all about how much you benefit from the home delivery services. It adds value to the products you buy. This story is reinforced by companies who tell you that they got rid of plastic bottles, by offering refills which they will deliver to you every week or month, omitting the fact that in doing so they will be increasing air pollution because of transportation.

Getting out of the comfort of home delivery requires the same effort as switching from virtual to real life. We have more control over the stories we create for ourselves than over our own real lives. When things don't go our way, we can change the story but it is harder to change our real lives. That is why we are often in denial and don't want to face reality as it is. It takes us to a state of cognitive dissonance because what we see, hear, and have to do is incompatible with what we want to see, hear, and do. Put in other words, the stories reality tells us are incompatible with the stories we create in our minds and this situation makes us very uncomfortable.

In some cultures, people will openly disagree with you and as uncomfortable as it would make you feel, you know that their comment is genuine because they live in a word-deed-valued culture. In some other cultures, people will agree with everything you say because disagreeing is rude, but their actions will be opposed to what they say because they think the opposite of what they said.

If we want to make progress, we should learn from the past because nothing makes sense without a context. History is here to teach us and make us understand and evolve. Rather than removing or changing the past, we should learn from it to avoid making the same mistakes. If you remove the past, you don't understand the present and can't plan the future.

Ironically, the more things change, the more they stay the same. We are still opposing people from different races to each other, we are still opposing women to men, and we like violent entertainment just like the Romans did in their "circus". And if you see things a bit differently or are clairvoyant, you are a called a complotist and deserve to be canceled just like the "witches" were burned in the Salem witch trials back in the 17th century.

Countries try to expand their territories and impose their culture and religion while hi-tech companies created global empires imposing new communication habits to all the peoples. In reality, each community tries to take over others and impose their own culture and habits. That is the opposite of multiculturalism. Slavery still exists, and in several countries there are people killing people just because they don't believe in the same God. Nothing has really changed since the old times. Actually, nothing was learned by the intelligent ape called *Homo sapiens*.

Multicultural marketers play an important role in respecting cultural differences. Rather than globalizing, the multicultural marketer should pay respect to different cultures by designing a specific marketing strategy to address each one of the different cultural targets in this multicultural world. Rather than replicating what goes against multiculturalism, marketers should celebrate multiculturalism through their products, by enticing consumers to embrace stories that provide them with something new and exciting such as getting to better know their culture and others' cultures too. Multicultural marketers have the responsibility of satisfying people by making their lives better. This goal can only be reached if consumers see all the benefits of belonging to a multicultural world.

APPENDIX

Food for Thought— Additional Notes From My LinkedIn Articles Used in My Research

www.LinkedIn.com/in/ElianeKarsaklian

#Talent first

So many talented people come to me to share their frustrations: life is unfair. They feel like they are unable to stand out and to be acknowledged because they don't have the right #network and are so busy doing their job that they wouldn't spare time for self-promotion. Indeed, we always see the same few people invited everywhere. Fame attracts #fame and money makes money.

I try to help talented people in my job as a professor, a researcher, and a consultant. I have seen bright researchers being turned down because they are not in the right network. As a professor, I see some students do a great job, want to learn and contribute ideas, whereas others play the know-it-all while contributing much less just to draw attention to themselves. As a consultant, I see companies only reaching out to people who are well known and have already worked with other companies.

We live in a world of personal praise, rather than talent #value. Hard workers, talented people who are the backbones of companies are rarely seen. They stay in the background. They too want to shine, but feel as if they can't compete with videos of cats, dancing, and selfies from dangerous places, because no one cares about content. No wonder why everyone wants to be a celebrity and it has been made so much easier with social media.

That is why I am calling to Talent First. Let's open the door to unknown talented people. Let's give them the opportunity to enlighten our minds with their #knowledge. Let's give five stars to people who don't portray themselves like a star.

You know it, but can you explain it?

Anyone living #abroad can tell about behavioral differences between their home and host #countries. But can they explain the underlying reasons for such differences?

That is my job: helping to understand #cultural differences and how to cope with them.

Where did #criticalthinking go?

We need to give people things to think about without telling them what to think.

We get #information already processed and summarized everywhere and think that that's it. We don't check the #sources, we don't check the #facts. Worse, we don't analyze it.

And if it is too long, we just ignore it.

How can we conduct #successfulbusiness without analyzing?

How can we conduct #internationalbusiness without understanding?

Then, we are surprised when hundreds of companies fail internationally every month.

#Companies fail because of conceptual #inacuracy

The number of misuses of #business terms and concepts is growing as companies create their own jargon and spread it out to the market. By using the same words to define different things, conceptual inaccuracy is detrimental to companies and young professionals alike.

There is confusion between #turnover and #revenues, the last one being broader than the first one. #Benchmark is often used with the meaning of #competitive analysis, although these are two different activities with specific roles in a company

In a #swotanalysis, strengths, opportunities and objectives are all mixed up as are #weaknesses and #threats.

#D&I is preached everywhere as if they were part of the same concept. Yet, you can have #diversity without #inclusion.

#Ethnicity/race are often proposed as one of the demographic criteria in defining populations as if they were the same thing. Ethnicity is a #cultural construct while #race is a biological one. There is no link between both.

#Panel is used instead of #sample when results of surveys are presented. These are two different sampling methods.

The lack of accuracy leads to inaccuracy in the measurement of the outcomes, in the establishment of objectives and consequently to flawed #strategicplanning.

Trapped in this jargon created and sustained by companies, media and blogs, young professionals get confused and feel pressured to embrace a new and inaccurate vocabulary despite what they learned at school.

——

Are you upset when #competitors copy your #concept ?

You should rather feel flattered because that means that your concept is good and that there is a demand for it.

This also means that the #market is growing and thus there are more opportunities for everyone.

But some companies will complain to everyone to start a negative word of mouth against their competitors. Others will proceed with a lawsuit.

Instead of wasting time, energy and money being upset, real #leaders plan ahead. Make sure you keep earning the biggest market shares, count on your #customers' loyalty and have your innovations ready to go both in your domestic market and #internationally. This is the secret for your company's longevity.

——

Pick the #right apples.

A rotten apple can spoil a whole basket of apples.

But a good apple cannot fix a basket of rotten apples.

Let's remember this in our leadership, management and marketing decisions.

——

Customer #loyalty

You have a great product and a bad #service; your clients will go away.

You have an average product and a great service; your clients will stay.

You have a great product and a great service; your clients will bring you new clients.

What your customers want is to have a great experience.

Why did I #learn to drink coffee?

I had never liked coffee. I am a tea drinker. But I had to learn to drink coffee for the good of my professional life.

In some countries, when meeting in offices, I was just poured coffee without any questions.

In some others, they would ask me if I wanted coffee without giving me any other options.

And in some other countries, they would ask me what I would like to drink. Whenever I would ask for a cup of tea, I would create a situation: Do we have tea? Where can we boil water...? I would deeply regret my request.

In some restaurants, they would serve coffee to all guests at table. Whenever I asked for tea it would come after everyone had already finished their coffee, and I would feel embarrassed for making everyone else wait for me.

It was better to learn to drink coffee; a little effort worth to make my international life much easier. I still don't like it, but it is one less barrier to think about.

———

I don't agree with your #opinion

Of course, an opinion is personal and it doesn't leave room to agreements or disagreements. Just like facts; they are what they are whether we like them or not. I can expose my opinion too, but should respect yours.

But if what you say is an assumption, then I can counter argue based on facts.

You can also disagree with my beliefs, my religion and my art. That means that you disagree with my #culture. It is a waste of time. Each culture is different and there is no right or wrong in these differences.

"I disapprove of what you say, but I will #defend to the death your right to say it" (Evelyn Hall 1976).

———

Don't be the common #enemy

Do you know these people who are so angry at themselves that they are always looking for a fight with anyone? They are everywhere. And because they are aware of their own limitations, they act surreptitiously, gathering other people they will use as shields.

After a while, they do such a good job that you are hated by people who barely know you. This is what we call the "common enemy" in #negotiations . You are attacked by people who feel threatened by you. If you fight back, you are more likely to be trapped in a fight without even knowing why you are there and who exactly you are fighting. This will make you weaker because of all the time and energy you will be dedicating to this fight you never wanted. Also, it will get you distracted from your own goals, which, if you continue pursuing, you will continue threatening them with your great performance.

You need to be wiser than them and just keep doing your job with the same consciousness and excellence. If you don't fight back, there is no fight, they will lose interest and look for another enemy easier to beat than you.

———

Here is why you should #travel

If you think that you can keep living on #Zoom, think again.

You will miss the travel #experience which widens the horizons, enables incomparable human connections and promising business partnerships. It also shows you that what happens in your country is not necessarily transferable to others.

No jet lag or long haul can be as tiring as Zoom fatigue. The former are ephemeral while the latter sticks with you.

Can Netflix replace going out to the movie theater?

Can your own Nespresso machine replace the pleasure of going to a coffee house?

Can homemade cocktails and food replace the restaurant and bars' experience?

Is watching games on TV the same as experiencing them in the stadium?

Does online networking replace in person events?

So how could online platforms replace traveling?

—————

Shame of #flying

Half of the food you consume comes from other countries and generates millions of jobs. These products are transported along with passengers on planes; no additional CO_2 footprint. For instance, in Kenya only, the export of flowers represents 800 million dollars and 2 million jobs.

A plane consumes 2.3 liters (0.608 gallons)/100 km (62.14 miles), much less than most cars. A car with one passenger's footprint is 95 g (0.29 lb)/100 km (62.14 miles) of CO_2, same as for a plane. While airlines count for 22% of CO_2 footprint, IT counts for 4% and clothing for 10% for the production only (add transportation to both).

Boycotting aviation on behalf of anti-pollution initiatives won't reduce the CO_2 footprint and will make more people than you could imagine lose their jobs.

#aviation #transportation #export

—————

What to do with #culturally unaware people?

I've always been mocked because I've always been a foreigner (even in my own country) for having been living across countries ever since I was born. That explains why I have a different perspective to things and life and why I certainly do things differently. I am a mix of several cultures, thus, wherever I go I am the weirdo.

It hurt because I took it personally until I understood that the issue was not me.

When people laugh at me I just say "well, if it makes you happy, it is already worth it. Now let me explain why I do things differently. If it helps to widen your horizon, it will be twice worthwhile".

———

#Product-centric and #Customer-centric approaches

If you are confused about companies' strategies to a market, think like this:

Product-centric companies address the needs they think consumers have.

Customer-centric companies address consumers' wants.

Both are valid strategies but the company should know how to deliver to the market in order to avoid rejection of their products.

———

Going Backwards

Born multicultural and raised across continents, I dedicated my whole life to bringing people from different cultures together. It was tough at the beginning because business people wouldn't believe in cultural differences. But, with the development of #internationalbusiness and #expatriation, companies were urged to take cultural differences seriously. Thus, biculturals were highly valued because they could naturally navigate between two cultures. We had made a lot of progress, at last.

#Multiculturalism is built on collaboration, willingness to adapt, respect of others and on trust building. Yet, the new rule is opposition and breaking the rules became the new normal. We are encouraged to be self-centered with no cultural curiosity at all. People are defined by the color of their skin, gender and sexual orientation. It all became personal: if you are not like me you are against me. This increases the likelihood for biculturals to be rejected by both sides.

Decades of academic research, development of study abroad and international exchange programs, and intercultural trainings aiming at creating generations of people open to diversity are going down the drain because few unaware and exclusionary people think that they are better off in a monocultural world.

———

All lives matter. Literally

Our planet is falling apart, our fauna and flora are dying and our children are being shot. There is urgency and yet all our attention is channeled towards the destruction of statues of people who supported and practiced slavery when, as inhuman as it could be, was a legal and accepted practice. Irony, active protesters wear clothes and shoes manufactured by the 21st century's slaves and so are the devices they use to document riots. In doing so, they support today's illegal slavery; children, women, men, of all colors of skin, cramped in one room where they live and work 24/7.

This is what is worth fighting for. We are all from the same race; the human race. And we are destroying ourselves and our home. Isn't it time to focus on our current and future challenges rather than being dragged down by the past? We can't change the past, but we can learn from it and shape the present and future of our children, of ALL peoples of this world and of our planet. We need to stop being short-sighted by controlled information and work towards sustainability in our relationships with others and with our planet. Or our legacy won't be anything to be proud of either.

———

The #decisionmaking conundrum

There is no right decision.

Anyone who has ever got married, raised a child or ran a company knows that. Also those who gave in to an impulsive purchase, who trusted someone else with a secret or followed some advice from internet know that.

All decisions are both right and wrong. The right side is all the reasons that lead us to make that decision. The wrong side is the consequences we face later on.

Decision making is managing trade-offs. All the good and the bad are to be balanced. We want progress without pollution and we want internet without information control and yet we know that this is not how it works. But do we know how good are the decisions we are making today? Are we really able to foresee the repercussions of our current decisions? We need to think about what we are giving away to get what seems to be important today.

———

The curse of #accuracy

When traveling across countries, the only certainty is that challenging surprises in professional settings are likely to happen.

I was invited to a business lunch as it happens very often but this time, rather than having been taken to a restaurant, I was taken to a food truck!

And once, someone invited me for a coffee but brought his own tumbler to the coffee house!

Having been invited to a black tie party, I carried a long dress in my bag only to be told, in situ, that it was actually a very informal party. People would even show up in blue jeans.

While in some other country, I was taken from work directly to an official and formal reception in an Embassy just wearing my work clothes. That one was really embarrassing!

As disruptive as these situations can be, you need to understand that words don't carry the same meaning and just play along. When working internationally you need to be prepared to everything as surprising as it can be.

———

Storytelling and the new #followers

#Storytelling is as old as mankind. It would bring people together around the campfire where someone would tell a story. The more mysterious, adventurous and unlikely the story was, the more popular was the storyteller. And this is how beliefs were created and passed on to the following generations.

No one could ever tell lie from truth because there were no writings and no ways of checking the facts. There was faith in what was said.

Today, the storytellers are in politics, marketing, leadership and everywhere on social media. Although there are so many ways to check the truth through factual proofs, people react immediately to the stories and make them true by the number of likes, reshares and followers. Once these figures go up, everyone is expected to follow the mob, because if they show facts that contradict the settled beliefs, they are marginalized. Even when they are right.

Storytelling is powerful because it addresses emotions. You can't manipulate reason, but you can take people wherever you want them to go through their emotions. And this is how new beliefs are created. And people just follow them with no questioning.

The only difference with the old times is that the reach of storytellers went from dozens to millions of people.

———

When we were #wrong

There was a time we thought the Earth was the center of the Universe. We didn't know about subatomic particles, we couldn't understand the electromagnetic field, and anything heavier than air would never fly. We would die at early ages because we didn't know all illnesses and we had no medicine or vaccines. Also, we believed in witches and burned them; we had slaves, in all countries and in all colors of skin, and women wouldn't go to school or vote.

All this is part of our #history. It did happen and nothing we can do today will change what has happened. But it is because we understood the flaws of what we did that we evolved. It is because we started doing things differently that we created progress. Had we erased the past or negated what had happened, how could we be better today?

Progress is doing better than what has been done before. If we do the same things we criticize, it is no progress. It is going back to when what we did was wrong.

———

#Revenge Shopping

This new definition of shopping comes along with shops reopening after the pandemic. Most predictions about the #newnormal were betting on an increase of online shopping but they didn't take into account humans' need for socializing. Some studies showed that the pandemic brought 46% of new online buyers but online shopping started decreasing as soon as the shops reopened.

Among the big winners of the lock down were grocery shops and webinars. Groceries' prices as well as home delivery including tips went significantly up. And the most valuable asset webinars brought to companies was data. Participants would disclose their contact information, participate in polls and fill out questionnaires about their businesses. In the "interest of time" free webinars would give a quick snapshot of the topic and direct attendees to the company's website where they would be charged to know more.

Most companies neglect the pleasure-shopping such as picking their own produce, touching the fabric and trying clothes on. The immediate benefit obtained by shopping in stores outweighs the downside of the delayed benefit linked to online shopping for some products. More importantly, consumers lose all the influence of atmospherics when shopping online. Shopping is hedonistic.

––––––

Future adults will be fearful, suspicious and D&I averse.

We might be doing the right thing but what are our #children taking away from this? Recently they were told not to go to school, not to play with their friends, not to visit their grandparents because a foreign virus was killing people out there. Now we are telling them that the bad guys kill the good guys who don't look like them. These children are likely to feel safe only around people who look like them and grow suspicious of everyone else. They will carry those beliefs out to adulthood and behave accordingly.

We are showing our children how unsafe the world is for those who are different. We can keep talking about racial #discrimination forever but the only action that can disrupt the segregation trend is education.

The understanding of #multiculturalism should start in the early ages. Family and school should lead the way to the understanding of its benefits without favoring or stigmatizing any race. It would help if the media and politicians stepped aside.

To change things we need to change our discourse and help our children to build a better world with less ignorance and more rationality. Otherwise, we'll be perpetuating the situations we claim to be against today.

Burning down places, vandalizing stores and fighting on the streets can only lead to more drama.

The more race and color of skin will be highlighted in these situations, the more we will witness the escalation of #racial discrimination. We need to claim the end of humans killing humans no matter who they are if we want to reach #peace and D&I in this world.

———

From head count to #dead count

Since the beginning of the #covid_19 crisis, all we see are figures of deaths per country. It turned into a kind of daily competition where the smallest figure was supposed to win however the spotlight is on the biggest numbers including the scandals involving nursing homes.

Have you noticed that no journalists write about how to save those who are still alive in nursing homes? Don't count on them to help to save lives. There is no sensationalism in saving lives. They look for losses.

If a member of your family is mistreated or contaminated in a nursing home and you try to denounce it in the media, you are wasting your time. Journalists couldn't care less, but they will most certainly want to interview you when your relative dies so that your case can add on their numbers.

———

What is the #New Normal"?

The "new normal" has been presented as life after the #covid19.

Before trying to define the new normal shouldn't we first define "normal"? Who says that the lives we had before the pandemic were normal?

Aren't we speaking here about "new usages" based on our past usual rather than normal?

Wouldn't the right term be the "new usual"?

The main question would be how we transition from a virtual (remote) life to a real life?

This is a good time for introspection. We need to understand what we have been missing out before and during the crisis.

What do you miss the most now; your virtual friends or your real friends?

What kind of time will you enjoy the most when this is over; the virtual time or the real time?

This is an invitation to reflect about the values of virtual and real.

#next #transition #normal

———

Like Expats during the #covid19

Being far away from family and friends is something expats are used to. Communicating remotely too. Also missing all the gatherings, celebrations and parties. If you feel like that because you are confined, you are sampling what all expats feel all the time.

Also they can't always share a remote meal with their families or happy hours with their friends because of the time difference. If living away from family and friends is one of the main reasons of dissatisfaction, depression and early reentry, these feelings are accentuated during the lock-down.

Travel ban, distance, concerns about the elderly can lead expats to regret having accepted to live abroad. Thus, demands for repatriation are increasing and jeopardizing their relationship with both the home and host companies—family comes first!

The feeling of isolation experienced by all those who are confined is exacerbated when it comes to expats. One consequence for those who stay in the host country is the increased consumption of products from the home country.

———

Before this #pandemic, we were all brothers and sisters across countries and cultures.

Then, Asian-looking people started to be stigmatized and set apart. Then, the tension in Europe started to escalate. Italy accusing France and Germany of lack of help, France threatening the UK because of their policy to contain virus spread, and Germany being the first one closing the borders.

Those countries, previously committed to cooperate no matter what, are now looking inwards and protecting themselves from their neighbors, nationalizing their companies and asking their citizens to buy local rather than European.

Where did all the preached tolerance, openness to others, and multiculturalism go? As they say, it is when you are in trouble that you see who your real friends are.

It's worse outside.

During the #staysafestayhome policy the best thing you can do is to stay at home. If you feel depressed at home, you might feel even worse when you go outside.

Shops are closed and the few people walking around look down and avoid you. There is no vibe at all on the streets. And if you go grocery shopping, you might end up buying what you don't need because what you need is not there.

We can't wait to see our cities as vibrant places as before and this moment might come sooner rather than later. But going out right now is not the best option to cheer anyone up.

We are better off at home doing what makes us happy!

References

Ang, S., L. Van Dyne, and C. Koh. 2006. "Personality Correlates of the Four-Factor Model of Cultural Intelligence." *Group and Organization Management* 31, no. 1, pp. 100123.

Becker, M., T.P. Scholdra, and M. Berkmann. 2022. "The Effect of Content on Zapping in TV Advertising." *Journal of Marketing.* https://doi.org/10.1177/00222429221105818.

Decartes, R. 1637. "Discours de la méthode pour bien conduire sa raison et chercher la vérité dans les sciences." In *Les Échos du Maquis*, April 2011.

Durkheim, E. 2011. *Durkheim on Religion: A Selection of Readings With Bibliographies and Introductory Remarks.* Google Books.

Earley, C. and S. Ang. 2003. *Cultural Intelligence. Individual Interactions Across Cultures.* Stanford University Press.

Goddard, D. 2022. Tao Te Ching Lao Tsu. King Solomon.

Goleman, D. 1995. *Emotional Intelligence.* Bantam Books.

Gottschall, J. 2012. *The Storytelling Animals.* Mariner.

Green, M. and T. Brock. 2000. "The Role of Transportation in the Persuasiveness of Public Narratives." *Journal of Personality and Social Psychology* 79, pp. 701721.

Hall, E. 1976. *Beyond Culture.* Anchor.

Harari, Y.N. 2015. *Sapiens. A Brief History of Humankind.* Harvill Secker.

Herz, M. and A. Diamantopoulos. 2017. "I Use It but Will Tell You That I Don't: Consumers' Country-of-Origin Cue Usage Denial." *Journal of International Marketing* 25, no. 2, pp. 52–71. https:doi.org//10.1509/jim.16.0051. ISSN 1069-031X (print) 1547-7215 (electronic).

Hofstede, G. 1984. *Culture's Consequences.* Sage.

Hofstede, G. and G.J. Hofstede. 2005. *Cultures and Organizations: Software of the Mind.* McGraw-Hill.

House, R.J., P.J. Hanges, M. Javidan, P.W. Dorfman, and V. Gupta. 2004. *Culture, Leadership and Organizations: The GLOBE Study of 62 Societies.* Sage.

Karsaklian, E. 1995. "La Mémorisation des Publicités par les Enfants." [Ph.D Dissertation], HEC Doctoral Program, France.

Karsaklian, E. 2012. "Using Brands to Overcome Culture Shock." *Australia and New Zealand Association of Management, Anzam Conference.* Australia.

Karsaklian, E. 2014. *The Intelligent International Negotiator.* Business Expert Press. ISBN-13: 9781606498064 (paperback). ISBN-13: 9781606498071 (e-book). ISSN: 19482752 (print). International Business Collection.

Karsaklian, E. 2016. "A Picture Can Be Worth a Thousand Stories. Interpreting Advertising Differently in 10 Countries." Journal of Marketing Development and Competitiveness 10, no. 2.

Karsaklian, E. 2017. *Sustainable Negotiation: What Physics Can Teach Us About International Negotiation.* Emerald Insight. ISBN: 9781787145764. eISBN: 9781787145757.

Karsaklian, E. 2019. The *After-Deal. What Happens After you Close a Deal.* Information Advertising Publishing. ISBN: 9781641138079.

Karsaklian, E. 2020. *The Negotiation Process. Before, During and After You Close a Deal.* Austin Macauley Publishers.

Karsaklian, E. 2020. "Openness to Diversity the Path to Multiculturalism? A Case Study Testing an Updated ODC Scale and the Influence of Social Desirability Bias." *International Journal of Multidisciplinary Perspectives in Higher Education* 5, no. 2, pp. 6685. ISSN: 2474-2546 Print/ ISSN: 2474-2554 Online https://ojed.org/jimphe

Karsaklian, E and Espinosa, J. 2021. "The Persuasive Process of Social Media News: An Adaptation of the Elaboration Likelihood Model of Persuasion." *International Society of Marketing Spring Conference.* United States.

Karsaklian, E. 2021. "Multiculturalism Needs More Than Openness to Diversity: Updating the Openness to Diversity and Challenge Scale for Increased Inclusion." *Journal of Cultural Marketing Strategy* 5, no. 2, pp. 184196.

Karsaklian, E. and E. Sauvage. 2023. "Between Standardization and Adaptation. An Analysis of the International Communication Campaign for Moët&Chandon Brand of Champagne." *Wine Marketing and Management.* Wiley.

Kotler, P. 1973. "Atmospherics as a Marketing Tool." *Journal of Retailing* 49, no. 4, pp. 4864.

Le Monde. n.d. www.lemonde.fr/planete/article/2021/01/20/paris-une-des-villes -ou-la-pollution-automobile-tue-le-plus-en-europe_6066860_3244.html.

Levi-Strauss, C. 1979. *Myth and Meaning. Cracking the code of Culture.* Schocken Books.

Lewis, R. 2006. *When Cultures Collide.* Nicholas Brealey.

Lewis, R. 2012. *When Teams Collide.* Nicholas Brealey.

Livermore, D. 2010. *Leading With Cultural Intelligence. The New Secret to Success.* Amacom.

Malhotra, N., D. Nunan, and D. Birks. 2017. *Marketing Research: An Applied Approach*, 5th ed. Pearson. www.pearsoned.co.uk/bookshop/detail.asp?item =100000000589380.

Maslow, A. 1943. "A Theory of Human Motivation." *Psychological Review* 50, no. 4, pp. 370–396.

Mauss, I.B., N.S. Savino, C.L. Anderson, M. Weisbuch, M. Tamir, and M.L. Laudenslager. 2012. "The Pursuit of Happiness Can Be Lonely." *Emotion* 12, no. 5, pp. 908–912. https://doi.org/10.1037/a0025299.

McLuhan, H.M. 1966. Information Theory. Google Books.

Moorman, C., M. Ryan, and N. Tavassoli. 2022. "Why Marketers Are Returning to Traditional Advertising." Harvard Business Review. https://hbr.org/2022/04/why-marketers-are-returning-to-traditional-advertising.

Pascarella, E.T., M. Edison, A. Nora, L.S. Hagedorn, and P.T. Terenzini. 1996. "Influences on Students' Openness to Diversity and Challenge in the First Year of College." *The Journal of Higher Education* 67, pp. 174–195. http://dx.doi.org/10.2307/2943979.

Petty, R.E. and J.T. Cacioppo. 1986. "The Elaboration Likelihood Model of Persuasion." *Advances in Experimental Social Psychology* 19, pp. 123205.

Rapaille, C. 2007. *The Culture Code*. Broadway Books.

Rogers, A., N.S. Harris, and A.A. Achenbach. 2020. *Neanderthal-Denisovan Ancestors Interbred With a Distantly Related Hominin. Science Advances* 6, no.,8. https://doi.org/10.1126/sciadv.aay548.

Salavoy and Mayer. 1990. "Emotional Intelligence." Journal of *Imagination, Cognition, and Personality*.

Schwartz, S.H. and W. Bilsky. 1987. "Toward a Universal Psychological Structure of Human Values." *Journal of Personality and Social Psychology* 53, pp. 550562.

Storr, W. 2020. *The Science of Storytelling*. Abrams Press.

Storti, C. 1999. *Figuring Foreigners Out. A Practical Guide*. Intercultural Press.

Trompenaars, F. and C. Hampden-Turner. 2006. *Riding the Waves of Culture. Understanding Cultural Diversity in Business*. Nicholas Brealey.

Walker, C.M. and T. Lombrozo. 2016. *Explaining the Moral of the Story*. Cognition. http://dx.doi.org/10.1016/j.cognition.2016.11.007.

Walker, D., T. Walker, and J. Schmitz. 2003. *The Guide to Cross-Cultural Success: Doing Business Internationally*. New York, NY: McGraw-Hill.

Warren, B. 2019. "Ancient Proteins Tell Their Tales." *Nature* 570, pp. 433436.

Wilson, D.S. 2003. *Darwin's Cathedral*. University of Chicago Press.

About the Author

Eliane Karsaklian, PhD, HDR, is an unusual combination of big picture thinker, academic, and practical businessperson. She has lived and worked in a number of countries during her career and mastered five languages, giving her extensive knowledge and experience in negotiation techniques and intercultural relationships. As an internationally known speaker and award-winning researcher, Dr. Karsaklian is invited as speaker at a number of universities around the world. She is currently clinical professor at the University of Illinois Chicago. Her more recent book—*The Negotiation Process. Before, During and After You Close a Deal*—introduces a completely new perspective to international negotiation, providing practical, field-tested examples, first-hand experience and guidance to enable readers to implement sustainable negotiation in the real world. For more, visit www.LinkedIn.com/in/ElianeKarsaklian

Index

OTHER TITLES IN THE MARKETING COLLECTION

Naresh Malhotra, Georgia Tech, Editor

- *Marketing of Consumer Financial Products* by Ritu Srivastava
- *The Big Miss* by Zhecho Dobrev
- *Digital Brand Romance* by Anna Harrison
- *Brand Vision* by James Everhart
- *Brand Naming* by Rob Meyerson
- *Fast Fulfillment* by Sanchoy Das
- *Multiply Your Business Value Through Brand & AI* by Rajan Narayan
- *Branding & AI* by Chahat Aggarwal
- *The Business Design Cube* by Rajagopal
- *Customer Relationship Management* by Michael Pearce
- *The Coming Age of Robots* by George Pettinico and George R. Milne
- *Market Entropy* by Rajagopal
- *Decoding Customer Value at the Bottom of the Pyramid* by Ritu Srivastava
- *Qualitative Marketing Research* by Rajagopal
- *Social Media Marketing* by Alan Charlesworth
- *Employee Ambassadorship* by Michael W Lowenstein

Concise and Applied Business Books

The Collection listed above is one of 30 business subject collections that Business Expert Press has grown to make BEP a premiere publisher of print and digital books. Our concise and applied books are for...

- Professionals and Practitioners
- Faculty who adopt our books for courses
- Librarians who know that BEP's Digital Libraries are a unique way to offer students ebooks to download, not restricted with any digital rights management
- Executive Training Course Leaders
- Business Seminar Organizers

Business Expert Press books are for anyone who needs to dig deeper on business ideas, goals, and solutions to everyday problems. Whether one print book, one ebook, or buying a digital library of 110 ebooks, we remain the affordable and smart way to be business smart. For more information, please visit www.businessexpertpress.com, or contact sales@businessexpertpress.com.

www.ingramcontent.com/pod-product-compliance
Lightning Source LLC
Chambersburg PA
CBHW061315220326
41599CB00026B/4882